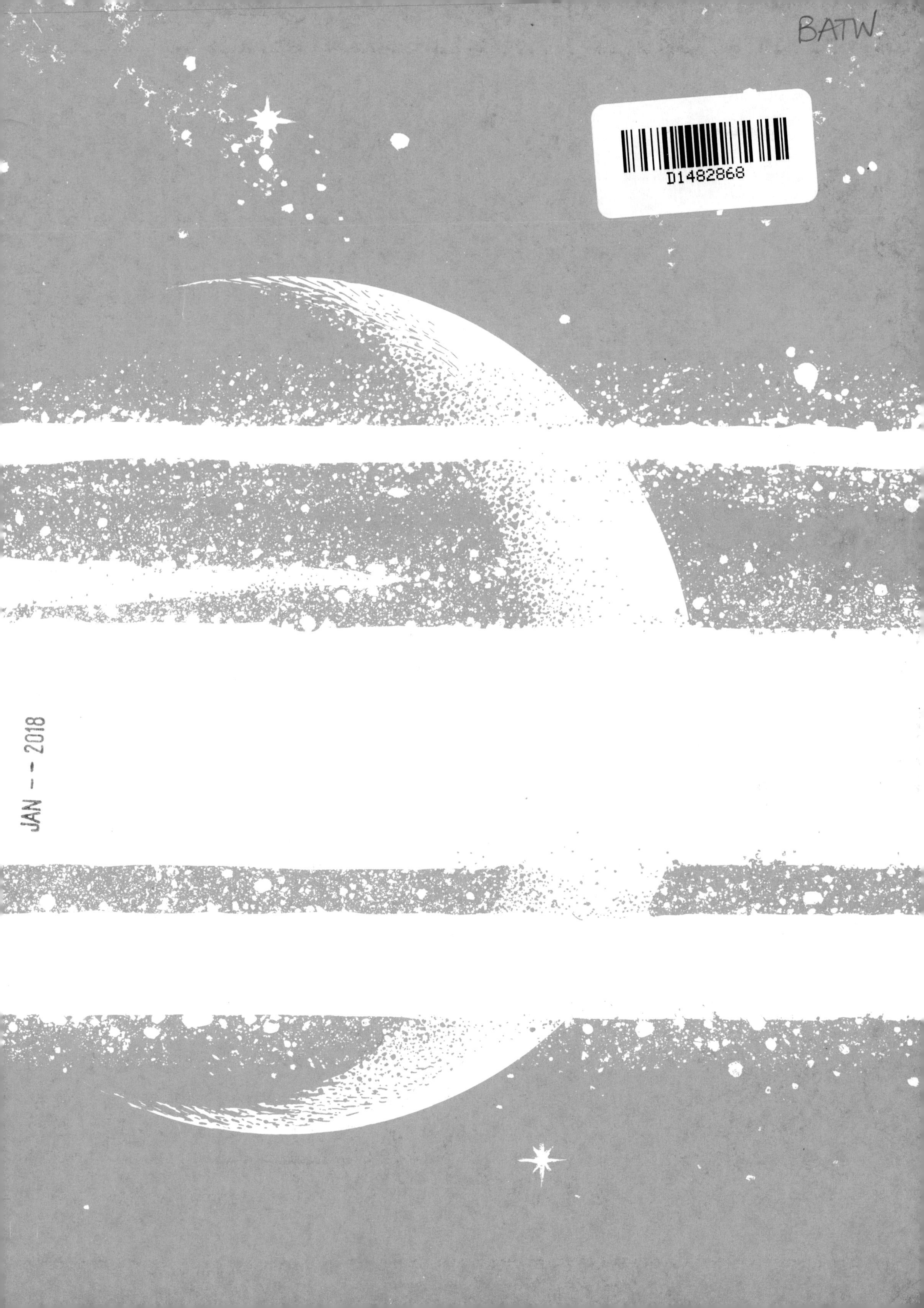

CHRISTIN   MÉZIÈRES

VALERIAN

THE COMPLETE COLLECTION VOLUME 1

9th CINEBOOK
The 9th Art Publisher

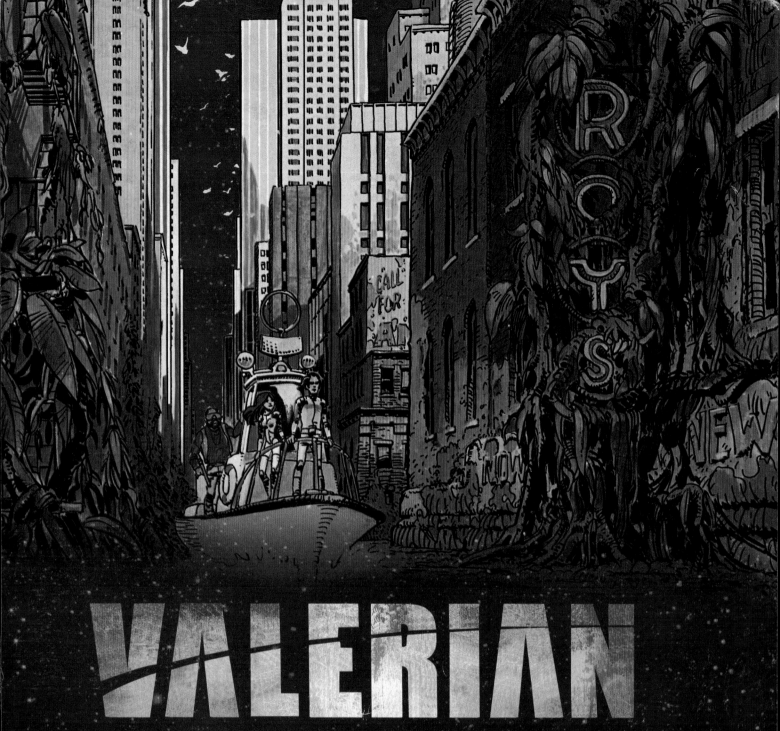

VALERIAN

THE COMPLETE COLLECTION VOLUME 1

SCRIPT **PIERRE CHRISTIN**   ARTWORK **JEAN-CLAUDE MÉZIÈRES**

COLOURS ÉVELYNE TRANLÉ

9th CINEBOOK
The 9th Art Publisher

Original title: Valerian – L'Intégrale Volume 1
Original edition: © Dargaud Paris, 2016 by Christin, Mezières & Tranlé
www.dargaud.com
All rights reserved
English translation: © 2016 Cinebook Ltd
Translator: Jerome Saincantin
Lettering and text layout: Design Amorandi
This edition first published in Great Britain in 2017 by
Cinebook Ltd
56 Beech Avenue
Canterbury, Kent
CT4 7TA
www.cinebook.com
Second printing: May 2017
Printed in Spain by EGEDSA
A CIP catalogue record for this book
is available from the British Library
ISBN 978-1-84918-352-9

INTERVIEW LUC BESSON, JEAN-CLAUDE MÉZIÈRES AND PIERRE CHRISTIN (PART 1)

BY CHRISTOPHE QUILLIEN

IN AN EXCLUSIVE AND PREVIOUSLY UNPUBLISHED INTERVIEW CONDUCTED FOR THIS NEW COLLECTED EDITION OF *VALERIAN AND LAURELINE*, LUC BESSON, JEAN-CLAUDE MÉZIÈRES AND PIERRE CHRISTIN SHARE CONFIDENCES, SUCH AS BESSON'S CHILDHOOD CRUSH ON LAURELINE. LET'S MEET WITH A FILM MAKER AND TWO COMIC ARTISTS AS THEIR SHARED DREAM COMES TRUE AT LAST: TO SEE THE ADVENTURES OF THESE TWO ICONS OF THE NINTH ART TRANSLATED TO THE BIG SCREEN.

Jean-Claude Mézières, Luc Besson and Pierre Christin during filming.

Photo: Vikram Gounassegarin

Luc Besson, how did your desire to make *Valerian* into a film come about?

Luc Besson: I blame Pierre Christin and Jean-Claude Mézières! When I was ten, every week I'd read the adventures of Valerian in *Pilote*. Which was actually quite frustrating: I'd wait a whole six days for the magazine to come out, but once it was in my hands, I wouldn't read it right away. I'd wait an hour or two; I even hid the right-hand page so I wouldn't see the end by accident! And I have to confess that I was very much in love with Laureline, even though I quite liked Valerian.

Pierre Christin: Back then, *bandes dessinées* were made by 'old little boys' for young little boys. Girls were quite rare in the comics world! The weekly publishing rhythm helped give a story a solid anchoring in the readers' minds...

When I was a teenager, *The Yellow M*, an adventure of Blake and Mortimer, made a strong impression on me. I would stave off boredom by drawing yellow Ms everywhere around me while I waited for next week's episode!

Luc Besson: Years later I had the good fortune to meet Jean-Claude Mézières, then we worked together on *The Fifth Element*.

Jean-Claude Mézières: For almost a year!

Luc Besson: That was when we started talking about the possibility of one day seeing *Valerian* in cinemas. Jean-Claude kept telling me: 'If you like the series so much, why don't you adapt it?' But making such a film in the 1990s would have been impossible. Too many aliens, too many monsters, too many space stations in *Valerian*! It took the revolution brought along by James Cameron: when *Avatar* came out, I thought to myself that the technology to make it was perhaps finally there. I'd already written several drafts of an adaptation a few years before then, but it was *Avatar* that made things possible.

What are the difficulties specific to cinema?

Pierre Christin: In a comic you can tell a *Valerian* story in 48 pages, even if there are lots of characters. In a film it's not so easy to shoot a scene that takes place in several places and with many actors. Changes of locations are easy to handle in *bandes dessinées*, but a lot more difficult in a film.

Luc Besson: You can read a graphic novel in half an hour, whereas a film is usually between one-and-a-half and two hours long. So there comes a point where I have to 'blow up' the story in order to develop the book's themes another way. Every form of expression is different; if someone were to adapt *Valerian* for songs, the sequences would be three minutes long. If *Valerian* were a painting, you'd have to fit all the characters into one enormous picture.

Jean-Claude Mézières: A *Valerian* musical! Now that would be fun!

Luc Besson: Jean-Claude, I'll leave it to you to set that up if you like...

Pierre Christin: Actually, we don't really know how much time we spend reading a comic. The first read-through takes around half an hour, yes, but you can re-read that same book a hundred, two hundred times throughout your life, or just flip through it and read two or three pages. Overall, you spend more hours reading a BD than reading a novel – even those classic novels you re-read every couple of years.

What are the main differences between these two forms of expression?

Luc Besson: In film, the timing is set. A minute is the same for every spectator in the room – time passes at the same speed for everyone. You can't take your time, as you would with a book. A comic, now, that's different. When you finish reading the right-hand page, you take a last look at the left-hand one before turning it. The reader can bask in the pictures and the text; they can fully savour them one last time before moving on to the next page. In film, the spectator has a clock that goes tick-tock for two hours and they can't stop it! It's the whole difference between free style and imposed style. A reader is free to read at their own pace.

Pierre Christin: Another difference lies in the art. There are comics where the characters sometimes change slightly from panel to panel, which can disrupt the reading - I should mention that this is never the case in *Valerian*! That doesn't happen in film. The actors always have the same face.

Luc Besson: Sort of... Some actors look pretty bad when they show up on set in the morning! You have to wait until they get the make-up on before you truly recognise them. When I read the comics, I get the feeling that Jean-Claude gives Laureline's face varying degrees of attention. She's more seductive in certain scenes...

Jean-Claude Mézières: My artistic talents grow and wane like the moon - I have good and bad days!

Luc Besson: Sometimes I think you really love Laureline very much!

Jean-Claude Mézières: I try to love her all the time, but it doesn't always shine through... Some days I sit back from my current page and think *Hey, not bad - she looks pretty good here!*

Pierre Christin and Jean-Claude Mézières, what is your relationship with Laureline and Valerian?
Pierre Christin: The relationship we have with our characters is strange. Looking at Laureline, for example, it's a lot easier for me to let her speak spontaneously. Before I've had time to even think about the sentence she's about to say, I'm already typing it on my keyboard! Valerian is much more uptight. His contribution to the dialogues doesn't come naturally to me. It must be Laureline's feminine side that keeps me excited.

Dane DeHaan, Luc Besson and Cara Delevingne.

Photo: Daniel Smith

7

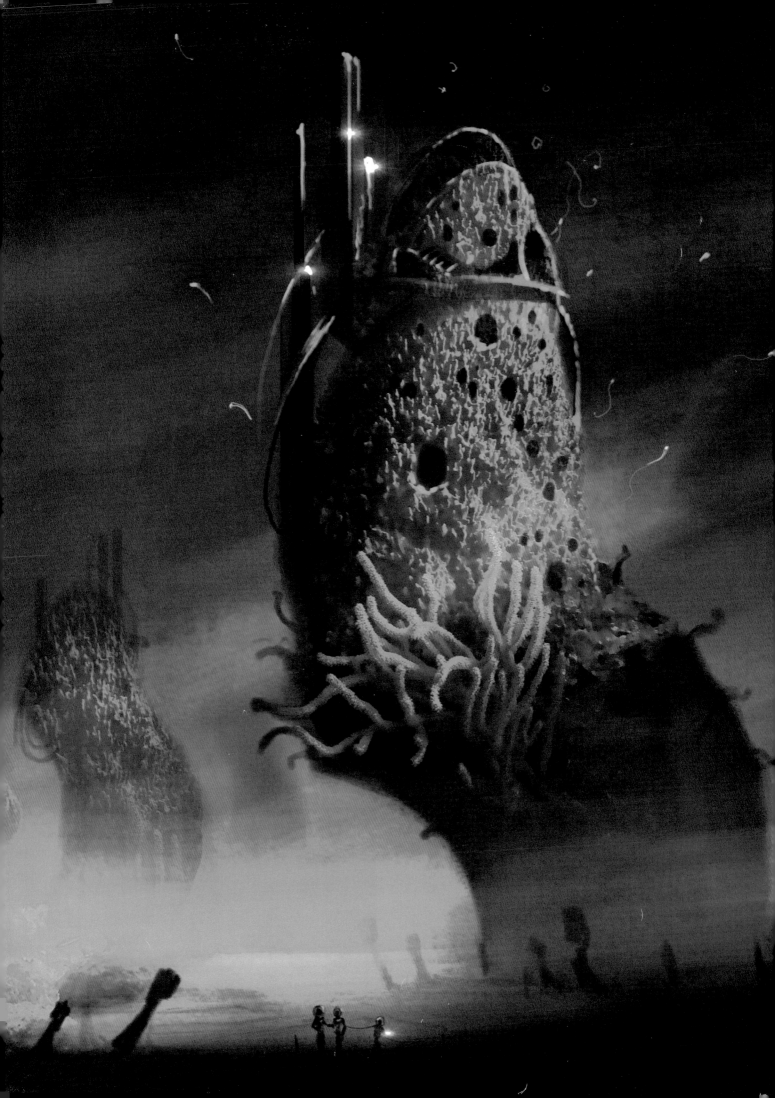

Luc Besson: Laureline is more ambiguous than Valerian. She has a problem with authority and a much more in-your-face attitude. Maybe because she has a different background – let's not forget she's from the Middle Ages.

Jean-Claude Mézières: The contrast between the two is one of the series' charms. Laureline is forever clashing with Valerian – she tends to rush into things.

Luc Besson, what sort of liberties are you taking with the characters in the film?

Luc Besson: I'm trying to remain faithful to their nature. And I haven't heard any complaints from the authors on that score... But characters talk much more in a film than in a comic book, so I'm forced to expand their lines of dialogue. Also, long-time readers of *Valerian* have known the nature of their relationship for a long time. But a first film is like a first book: some of the spectators won't know the series. So I went back to a time when Valerian and Laureline weren't together yet. Perhaps they're going to grow closer, perhaps not... It's an interesting situation to film.

Pierre Christin: It's funny – even before I knew how you'd be covering their relationship, I was hoping you'd do it this way. I think it's a very good thing to have the spectator wonder if anything will happen between them.

Jean-Claude Mézières: Some readers have reproached us for waiting until the tenth book before having them kiss... They're wrong, though. They kiss in their third adventure, *The Empire of a Thousand Planets*.

Luc Besson: Mostly they kiss between the pages...

Jean-Claude Mézières: A lot of things happen between the pages of a graphic novel!

Luc Besson: The first kiss I remember was in *Ambassador of the Shadows*.

Jean-Claude Mézières: I had a hard time drawing that panel. An artist can use a mirror to copy attitudes and expressions. But drawing while you're kissing is not very practical!

Luc Besson: You can ask your wife to help you...

Study for the transmuter

Jean-Claude Mézières: It's not that easy. It'd take three of us, and she'd need to be kissing someone else while I draw... I find kissing scenes horrible to draw!

Was Laureline inspired by a real person?

Jean-Claude Mézières: She's the incarnation of all the women I love. Since I'm not a good portraitist, she's not modelled on a former girlfriend – fortunately! She's more a representation of a type of woman than of a particular person.

Pierre Christin: We discussed the characters a lot, and Laureline is the result of both our tastes. I have to say – I liked her very much! Jean-Claude managed to create a heroine who was immediately a big hit and didn't change much over the course of the series.

GO WEST, YOUNG MEN !

To get away from such a gloomy, conformist world, Jean-Claude Mézières and Pierre Christin chose the West. America, here they come! A new culture, a new frontier! The former was slim and blond, the latter plump and dark-haired. One was an artist-in-training, dazzled by the open skies of the western genre. The other temporarily taught French literature in an American university. And as Christin confirms, it was to be their great voyage of discovery, fleeing the stuffiness of home to look for exotic inspiration and a new lease of life. And so, in 1965 in Salt Lake City – the old capital of the strict Mormons – the two young men met. Again, actually, as they'd known each other for 20 years. But this time life was ripe for the taking. And if we are to look for the precise moment when the *Valerian* saga was conceived, then why not imagine that the interstellar explorer was born there – at least on a subliminal level – in those wide open spaces where the two old friends could at last 'build a world in Technicolor'? At any rate, what a road it had been since the Val-de-Marne and Saint-Mandé! Precisely Saint-Mandé. That's where Mézières and Christin met, in the middle of the air-raid alerts of 1943–1944. When the sirens wailed, the neighbours would head down into the cellars to take shelter. The children, unaware of the danger and having fun, would play together. The first common memories were made then. Mézières tells this story: 'In a nearby school there was a group of little girls. One night, German trucks came to take them away. Much later I realised that they'd been Jewish refugees. They all disappeared...' That's an experience that can only be understood long afterwards. But that might also explain *Valerian*'s famously 'humanist' nature...

Mézières and Christin during their American period.
It was in the West that they created their first short stories for **Pilote**.

COLLIDING WORLDS

Mézières, the pictures man, spoke of Giraud, whom he'd met at the "Arts'A" (Applied Arts school), of Jijé, of Franquin and of that *Mad* magazine school whose virtuosity he admired. Add to that the poetry of wide open spaces, the songs of canyons and the crazy images of old B-movies such as *This Island Earth* or *Forbidden Planet*. Mix it all together, shake well, and something is bound to remain... As for Christin, the words man, he spoke of ideas and texts. His solid education (Paris Institute of Political Studies, and a PhD in literature) meant that he was at ease with a multitude of concepts. But he preferred imagination; a life dreamed rather than endured. He'd been among the first to discover science fiction, a literary genre still marginal at the time, confined in France to low-circulation magazines such as *Fiction* or *Galaxie*. But there, on American soil, he binged on Asimov and Van Vogt, on Vance and Wyndham. In their wake he rode comets and discovered the all-essential 'sense of wonder', that ability to be awed that seems as infinite as the universe itself. Everything was changing in America. The Civil Rights movement, the rise of feminism, the underground, the beatniks, the

From the very first panel of the first book, the stage is clearly set: 'Year 2720. Galaxity, capital of the Terran Galactic Empire.' Even though the treatment is still somewhat simple, it allows the imagination to soar.

emergence of rock music and all that burgeoning counterculture... And so everything was blended, stirred together, allowed to settle, and each one introduced the other to the days of first times and experimentations. On the other side of the Atlantic, there was *Pilote* magazine, where Goscinny reigned like a deus ex machina of the nascent modern *bandes dessinées*. They decided to send him their first attempts. Rather unexpectedly, they were published (which paid for the return tickets to France!). Mézières learned the ropes by illustrating some of author Fred's stories. Christin signed his first scripts under the pseudonym Linus.

Very soon, though, teaming up became the obvious move. And so we come to 9 November 1967.
In issue 420 of *Pilote*, readers discover *Bad Dreams*. The first panel is a view of Galaxity. By the second page, we meet a spatio-temporal traveller named Valerian. What about Laureline? Poor Laureline – she won't appear until page 11.
It's naive, even 'badly drawn'. But the series is already there. With all its basic principles.

EXPLORE ANYTHING, TELL ANY TALE...

Forty years later and the two men still haven't finished telling this epic story. Christin still finds it surprising sometimes: 'We made it like a couple of overgrown adolescents would. That story was for the fun of it.' The truth is that, even though Mézières likes to cite Barbarella – 'Laureline's spiritual grandmother' – and Christin acknowledges a debt to E.P. Jacobs and his 'fantastic elements set in a very realistic atmosphere', the pair broke new ground. To them we owe the introduction of modern science fiction into BD; an imaginary universe that can become a weapon to explore anything and tell any possible story. To Christin, it's evident: 'Science fiction was a fantastic way of "superheating" reality. It was the ideal vector for alluding to large-scale changes that were affecting our contemporary world and for describing our transition into modernity.'* It's hard to be any more explicit. Christin and Mézières are like storytellers from another world, passing on the knowledge of who we were and the idea of who we will be. With them, our fears echo through the emptiness of space. And 'that bestiary worthy of a galactic zoo, and those deliciously eclectic architectures'** always bring us back to Earth in the end, to speak to us about today, about all our problems called ecology, ideologies, feminism, totalitarianism... And about that humanism that always needs to be redefined.

*Interview by Patrick Gaumer in Les Années Pilote (1996)
**Gérard Klein, Des messagers de l'actuel. Une exploration des mondes de Valérian in Mézières et Christin avec... (1983)

'HELLO! THIS IS LAURELINE...'

In 2007, in later life, Christin and Mézières can look back on their creation: 40 years, over 20 titles and, in all, more than 2,500,000 volumes sold. Add translations into a dozen languages and an adaptation into an animated cartoon. The richness of their imagination, the luxuriant art, the omnipresent humour and satire also earned them the recognition of their peers, with an Angoulême festival Grand Prix for Mézières and a Prix Spécial from the European Science Fiction Society in 1987. As we said before, *Valerian* has become a classic. Even better, the series has truly become part of readers' lives. Nowadays, with a little luck, it's quite possible to meet a real Valerian or an authentic Laureline. According to census registers, the names have been given 1,852 and 2,062 times respectively since 1970. As Mézières tells it himself: 'Sometimes I'm at home, at my drawing board. The phone rings. I pick up and I hear "Hello! Hi, my name is Laureline..." Believe me, it's a damn good feeling!'

The metamorphoses of Laureline: in the space of three volumes, the young peasant girl from the Middle Ages turns into a '60s hippie, then into an ambassador of the future.

IMAGE CREATORS

Don't go thinking that there's nothing but philosophy in *Valerian*, though. It is, first and foremost, a visual world, and it's all too easy to forget just how innovative and groundbreaking it was. To best demonstrate that, allow me to tell a personal anecdote.

It was in 1977, during the International Science Fiction Festival that had seen the cream of the profession gather in Metz, France. Included in the film programme: the premiere of *Star Wars* in France.

At the end of the film, I remember Mézières laughing and telling me: 'It looked like an adaptation of *Valerian* for the big screen.'

After many long years of lethargy, *Star Wars* at last brought about the rebirth of American sci-fi cinema. Back then, Jean-Claude was already working on his seventh book. The series was well established. Valerian and Laureline had already explored the Thousand Planets, Alflolol, Point Central and many other strange worlds. Between the comic and the first episode of the film saga there was a clear kinship of *space opera*.

However, as years and *Star Wars* episodes went by, the kinship became more pronounced. Today, while Mézières has the obvious advantage of precedence, some settings, some scenes even, appear strangely similar.

Passing over the spaceships that seem to come out of the same assembly line, let's be charitable towards Princess Leia, who wears the same exotic outfits as Laureline (without ever having her charm). There are still other similarities, though. Han Solo frozen for all eternity

Welcome to Alflolol - 1972

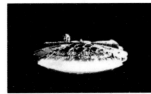

Star Wars - 1977

The Land Without Stars - 1972

Return of the Jedi - 1983

The Empire of a Thousand Planets - 1971

The Empire Strikes Back - 1980

The Empire of a Thousand Planets - 1971

Revenge of the Sith - 2005

The Empire of a Thousand Planets - 1971

Revenge of the Sith - 2005

Ambassador of the Shadows - 1975

The Phantom Menace - 2003

in a slab of translucent matter, like Valerian. Darth Vader hiding his burned face behind a sinister mask, like those of the Enlighteneds. Some 'funny' aliens in *The Phantom Menace* sporting both elongated snout and wings, like the Shingouz.

Is all this simple accident? Yes and no. By definition, the books are made to be sold far and wide, and we can't blame the *Star Wars* designers for gathering and using as much documentation as they could. But to the point that we'd be left with such coincidences? All creators thrive on influences, of course. Things, as the saying goes, are in fashion, and Mézières has become philosophical about it. He knows, though, that he is one of the fathers of modern science-fiction iconography, one of the main inspirations of that pool of images from which all later illustrators drank, consciously or not. It wasn't until 1997 that cinema finally gave credit to Jean-Claude Mézières, with Luc Besson's *The Fifth Element*, for which the artist did substantial work*. And let's not forget the eagerly awaited adaptation of *Valerian* by the same Luc Besson, due in 2017.

*For further details, see Les Extras de Mézières volume 2 - My Fifth Element, Dargaud.

THE STORIES IN THIS BOOK

'OUR FIRST BOOKS GIVE THE IMPRESSION THAT WE HESITATED JUST AT THE MOMENT OF TAKING FLIGHT. AS IF WE FIRST WANTED TO ESTABLISH OUR BASICS IN ORDER TO BE SURE OF WHERE WE CAME FROM. *BAD DREAMS* TAKES PLACE IN THE PAST. *CITY* EXPLORES THE PRESENT, WITH A PROPHETIC CATACLYSM. AND IT'S ONLY WITH *THE EMPIRE OF A THOUSAND PLANETS* THAT WE FINALLY DEPART, THAT WE HAVE LIFT-OFF.'
PIERRE CHRISTIN

BAD DREAMS – 1967

Valerian is sent by Galaxity to 11th-century France, chasing a dissident. While there, he encounters Laureline, who shows her pretty face for the first time ... and saves the young spatio-temporal agent from an early end! The saga begins with this first Valerian story that's almost like a draft. The action is sketchy, the art is still simplistic and the length is non-standard (which prevented publication as a book for a long time); but the humour, the situations and the characters are getting into place. The adventure can begin...

A science-fiction series that begins with a return to the Middle Ages... Right from the start, the temporal uncertainty characteristic of the saga is present.

THE CITY OF SHIFTING WATERS AND EARTH IN FLAMES – 1970

Cover of **Pilote** *announcing the publication of* **The City of Shifting Waters** *(1968)*

Valerian and Laureline arrive in New York in 1986, hunting for Xombul as he tries to take over after the cataclysm that devastated the planet. From the waters of the sunken city to the burning Yellowstone landscapes, a long chase begins... (The story appears in its full version here, the way it was pre-published in *Pilote*. The length of the two episodes – 2 x 28 pages – required several cuts to later fit standard book length). When they wrote this story in 1968 and placed the action in 1986, Christin had no way of knowing that 18 years later, in *The Ghosts of Inverloch* (1984), Valerian would find himself facing a painful time paradox. How to justify his continued activity even as Earth had been destroyed? We'll have ample opportunity to discuss that again... In the meantime, Christin takes the opportunity to symbolically return to the USA, origin of his inspiration, with this great cataclysm worthy of the best sci-fi novels, while Mézières begins to show the full measure of his talent. His images of a New York swallowed by sea and jungle, where seabirds - gulls and cormorants - flock are gorgeous. They count among the masterpieces of comic art.

Let's mention a rarity: two 'real' characters punctuate the story as a double bonus. Sun Rae is directly inspired by Sun Ra, jazz composer and piano player (1914-1993). As for the character of the scientist, he's both a caricature of Jerry Lewis (*The Nutty Professor*) and, through his name Schroeder, a nod to Schulz's *Peanuts* - a link that was already present, as at the time Christin was still signing his work under the pseudonym Linus!

THE EMPIRE OF A THOUSAND PLANETS – 1971

Syrte the Magnificent, capital of the Empire of a Thousand Planets! But on that bustling world, the ruling regime is shaky. Is power still in the hands of the imperial dynasty or has it already passed into those of the Enlighteneds, a mysterious priestly order? The Merchant Guild is worried. Valerian and Laureline investigate.

Mixing futurism and the Middle Ages, clearly drawing inspiration from traditional, Jack Vance-style space opera, this volume is the first 'great' *Valerian*, a symbol of the series taking flight. A true classic of BD, suffused with unequalled poetic charm. In that colourful atmosphere of strange cultures, guilds and decadent sects, Mézières delivers dazzling landscapes, equally skilful at describing dreary slums as at showing off the splendours of the imperial court. As for Christin, he indulges in lexical bliss. Walk in his footsteps and discover schamirs, spiglics, marcyams and stones of Arphal!

This volume also inaugurates a canonical structure that can be found in all the early books of the series: Valerian and Laureline come to a mysterious planet in the grip of war, strife and social oppression; of course, they play their part in ensuring good prevails. What if science fiction was just a pretext for a new humanism?

BAD DREAMS

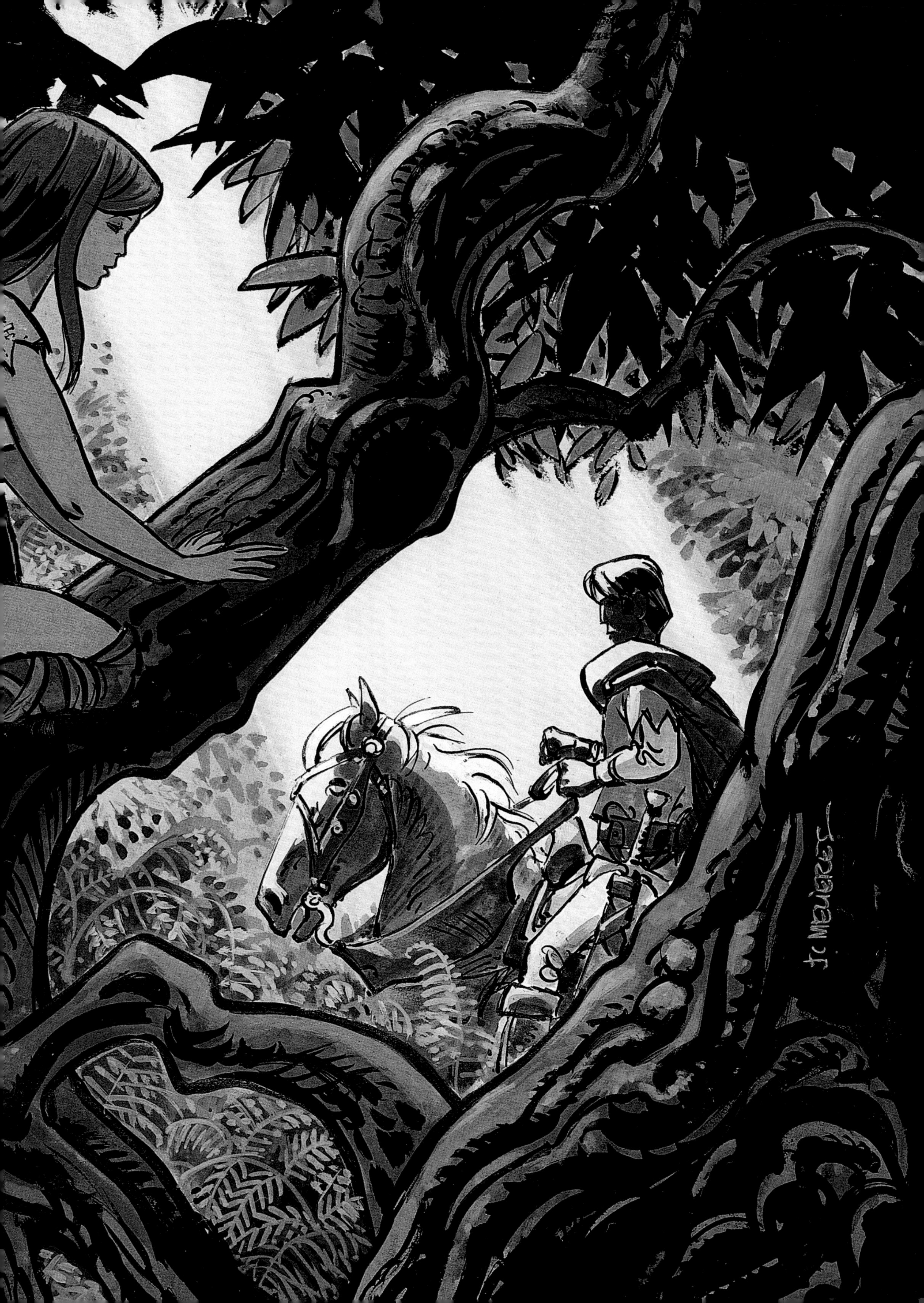

YEAR 2720. GALAXITY, CAPITAL OF EARTH AND THE TERRAN GALACTIC EMPIRE.

EVER SINCE THE INSTANT TELEPORTATION OF MATTER THROUGH TIME AND SPACE WAS DISCOVERED IN 2314, THE CONCEPT OF WORK HAS PRACTICALLY DISAPPEARED ON THE HOME PLANET.

ONLY A FEW HUNDRED AGENTS AND TECHNOCRATS OF THE SPATIO-TEMPORAL SERVICE STILL MAINTAIN AN ACTUAL PROFESSIONAL ACTIVITY.

THE AGENTS PATROL HISTORY TO SAFE-GUARD IT FROM TIME-TRAVEL PIRATES, AND EXPLORE DISTANT PLANETS TO SECURE NEW RESOURCES FOR EARTH.

THE TECHNOCRATS ARE SCIENTIFIC ADMINISTRATORS. THE MOST POWERFUL OF THEM, THOSE BELONGING TO THE FIRST CIRCLE, CONSTITUTE THE ONLY FORM OF PLANETARY OR INTERPLANETARY AUTHORITY.

AS FOR THE REST OF HUMANITY, IT INDULGES IN THE BLISSFUL HABIT OF DREAMING, UNDER THE CONTROL OF THE DREAMS DEPARTMENT, WHICH SCHEDULES THE PROGRAMS.

CIVILISATION SEEMS TO HAVE REACHED A POINT OF BALANCE. IT IS NOW 3.03 PM, STANDARD EARTH TIME...

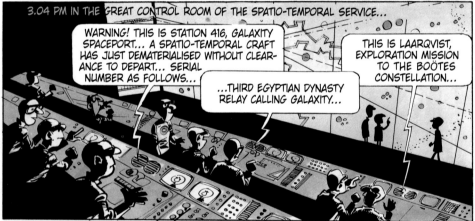

3.04 PM IN THE GREAT CONTROL ROOM OF THE SPATIO-TEMPORAL SERVICE...

WARNING! THIS IS STATION 416, GALAXITY SPACEPORT... A SPATIO-TEMPORAL CRAFT HAS JUST DEMATERIALISED WITHOUT CLEARANCE TO DEPART... SERIAL NUMBER AS FOLLOWS...

...THIRD EGYPTIAN DYNASTY RELAY CALLING GALAXITY...

THIS IS LAARQVIST, EXPLORATION MISSION TO THE BOÖTES CONSTELLATION...

3.06 PM, EARTH TIME, ON THE 18TH PLANET OF THE BINARY STAR ARCTURUS...

GALAXITY CALLING VALERIAN... SPATIO-TEMPORAL SERVICE CALLING VALERIAN...

?

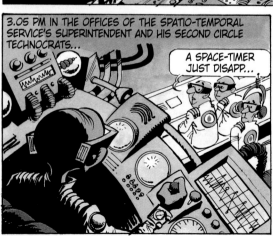

3.05 PM IN THE OFFICES OF THE SPATIO-TEMPORAL SERVICE'S SUPERINTENDENT AND HIS SECOND CIRCLE TECHNOCRATS...

A SPACE-TIMER JUST DISAPP...

I KNOW! JIRAD, CONTACT OUR BEST AVAILABLE AGENT IMMEDIATELY. LERKA, FIND ME THE NAME OF WHOEVER STOLE THAT CRAFT. IF HE GOT INTO THE SPACEPORT WITHOUT SPECIAL AUTHORISATION, THEN HE'S GOT TO BE A FIRST CIRCLE TECHNOCRAT. AND YOU, HELGOR, CONTACT THE CENTRAL COMPUTER AND FIND OUT IF ANY ANOMALIES HAVE BEEN DETECTED ANYWHERE...

GALAXITY CALLING...

RATS! SOUNDS LIKE I WON'T BE FINISHING MY MATHEMATICAL SCULPTURE ANY TIME SOON...

HA! THERE YOU ARE AT LAST! MUST YOU GO LAX WHEN YOU'RE OFF DUTY? BE IN MY OFFICE IN ... MMMM... SIX MINUTES EXACTLY. I NEED AN AGENT FOR A SENSITIVE MISSION... AND MAKE SURE YOU'RE IN UNIFORM – YOU KNOW I CANNOT ABIDE SLOVENLINESS...

GO SOFT? SHEESH! SIX MINUTES TO TRAVEL SEVERAL THOUSAND LIGHT YEARS AND PUT ON MY BEST UNIFORM... WELL, MIGHT AS WELL HURRY!

IT'S A GOOD THING MY SPACE-TIMER'S ON-BOARD COMPUTER CAN CALCULATE MY COORDINATES IN AN INSTANT... GOING HOME IS ALWAYS SIMPLE.

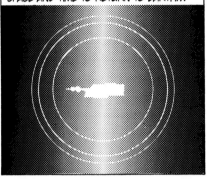

3.10 PM EXACTLY. AGENT VALERIAN, AS HE'S ALREADY DONE SO MANY TIMES IN HIS EVENTFUL LIFE, JUMPS THROUGH SPACE AND TIME TO RETURN TO EARTH...

AND AT 3.10 PM, JUST AS EXACTLY, HIS SPATIO-TEMPORAL CRAFT MATERIALISES IN GALAXITY SPACEPORT...

SHHHH

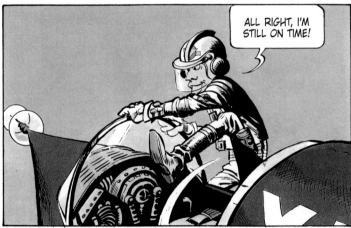

ALL RIGHT, I'M STILL ON TIME!

SPACE-TIME PARKING

3.12 PM...

LATE! BY TWO SECONDS! YOU'RE SLIPPING... BUT I'LL LET IT SLIDE, JUST THIS ONCE. THE SITUATION IS TOO SERIOUS, AND YOU'RE THE ONLY ONE WHO CAN GET US OUT OF IT...

...AND ACTUALLY THERE'S NO NEED TO WASTE ANY TIME HERE. THE CENTRAL COMPUTER HAS JUST REPORTED GRAVE DISRUPTIONS AT THE DREAMS DEPARTMENT. MIGHT AS WELL HEAD THERE PRESENTLY... JIRAD, IS MY PERSONAL BUBBLE READY?

IT'S WAITING FOR YOU, SIR!

JIRAD, HELGOR AND LERKA, COME WITH ME. I MIGHT NEED YOU. GET IN, VALERIAN. I'LL EXPLAIN WHAT HAPPENED ON THE WAY...

YES... AND THEN?

...WELL, PEOPLE HAD ALREADY BEEN COMPLAINING ABOUT THE POOR QUALITY OF THE DREAMS FOR SOME TIME. BUT WE'VE ONLY JUST FOUND OUT THAT THE CENTRAL COMPUTER'S PROGRAMING FOR THE DREAMS DEPARTMENT WAS COMPLETELY SABOTAGED ... AND THAT THE DREAMS SUPERINTENDENT ESCAPED IN A SPACE-TIMER...

THE VERY SAME! HE DEMATERIALISED PRECISELY ... MMM ... 13 MINUTES AGO. WE DON'T KNOW WHEN AND WHERE HE REMATERIALISED YET... GOOD! WE'RE ALMOST AT THE DREAMING HALL... LOOK!

WHO, XOMBUL?

WHAT'S WRONG WITH THEM?

COME NOW, VALERIAN! YOU KNOW VERY WELL THAT ALL TERRANS DO NOWADAYS IS DREAM. BUT WITH THE WHOLE NETWORK DISRUPTED, THEY'RE CUT OFF FROM THEIR FAVOURITE DREAMS AND FEELING EXTREMELY DISTRAUGHT. WHICH IS WHY WE MUST MOVE QUICKLY, BECAUSE WE DON'T KNOW HOW THEY MIGHT REACT... LET'S GO INTO A ROOM. ANY ROOM.

JIRAD, PICK A DREAM FOR US...

SOMETHING PASTORAL, SIR?

AS YOU WISH, AS YOU WISH...

OOOOOH! LOVELY!!!

BE QUIET AND WATCH, WILL YOU!!!

AHHHHH! MY FAVOURITE DREAM!

CLICK

24

MMMMH... DIVINE...

RAAH! SIR! THE ROSES!

OW! IT BIT ME!

SIR!

SIR! AAAAAAAH!!!

THANK YOU, VALERIAN. AND YOU, JIRAD! WHERE'S YOUR DIGNITY?! YOU KNOW AS WELL AS I DO THAT THESE ARE MERE THREE-DIMENSIONAL SENSORY ILLUSIONS – THERE'S NOTHING REAL HERE...

CLICK

SIR! SIR... BOOOHOOO

WHY DON'T YOU TAKE US TO THE CRYSTALLINE FORMATIONS OF ALDEBARAN? IT'S USUALLY A POPULAR DREAM, I BELIEVE...

CLIC

CLICK

SUCH HARMONY!...

MAGNIFICENT!!!

YES ... BUT IT LOOKS LIKE...

SIR!

AGAIN! THAT'S ENOUGH!

GOODNESS, JIRAD! YOU'RE RATHER EMO-TIONAL FOR A SECOND CIRCLE TECHNOCRAT. DO HAVE A SOOTHE-BUBBLE, MY BOY. IT'LL SET YOU TO RIGHTS.

A FINE MESS THAT XOMBUL HAS LEFT US! JUST LOOK AT THE STATE OF A SEASONED TECHNOCRAT LIKE JIRAD AND YOU CAN IMAGINE WHAT THE REST OF THE POPULATION IS LIKE. UNTIL THE PROGRAMS ARE RETURNED TO NORMAL, GALAXITY IS GOING TO BE THE CAPITAL OF NEUROSES!

I THINK THE BEST THING TO DO IS HEAD STRAIGHT TO XOMBUL'S HOME. MAYBE WE'LL FIND A CLUE, THE BEGINNING OF A LEAD...

AH! MUCH BETTER!

AND SO, A LITTLE LATER...

THIS IS WHERE HE LIVED.

WELL, WELL! XOMBUL HAD SOME ECLECTIC TASTES...

YOU KNOW, IT WASN'T FOR NOTHING THAT HE HEADED THE DREAMS DEPARTMENT. IT'S A JOB THAT CALLS FOR IMAGINATION... HAVE A LOOK AT ALL THIS STUFF WHILE I GO TO THE VIDEO ROOM AND CALL THE SERVICE TO SEE IF THERE'S NEWS...

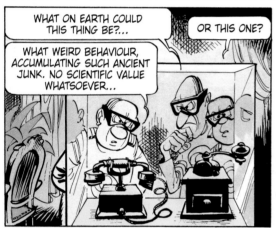

WHAT ON EARTH COULD THIS THING BE?...

OR THIS ONE?

WHAT WEIRD BEHAVIOUR, ACCUMULATING SUCH ANCIENT JUNK. NO SCIENTIFIC VALUE WHATSOEVER...

AND THAT???

SOME SORT OF MUSICAL INSTRUMENT, ISN'T IT?

A FAILED SCULPTURE, PERHAPS?

NO, GENTLEMEN. **THAT** IS A 20TH-CENTURY SEWING MACHINE! COME AND TAKE A LOOK AT THIS, THOUGH... I FOUND SOMETHING TOO! IT DOESN'T LOOK VERY SCIENTIFIC TO ME EITHER, BUT IT IS INTERESTING...

WHAT'S 'SO IN' ABOUT THIS MACHINE?

XOMBUL CERTAINLY LOVED EYESORES. LOOK!

WELL, I'LL BE! THIS DATES BACK TO AD 1000!!!

ARE THERE IMAGES?

THERE ARE, YES... BUT I DON'T THINK YOU'LL LIKE THEM. THIS MANUSCRIPT WAS WRITTEN BY ONE ALBERIC THE OLD AND IS ALL ABOUT SORCERY!

SORCERY!?! NO, THAT'S IMPOSSIBLE... OH, MY POOR NERVES!

SUCH NIGHTMARISH FIGURES!!!

EXCELLENT CHOICE OF WORDS ... AND I THINK I JUST FIGURED OUT WHERE XOMBUL WENT.

NO NEED TO FIGURE IT OUT, VALERIAN. I WAS JUST IN DIRECT CONTACT WITH THE AD 1000 TEMPORAL RELAY. AN UNIDENTIFIED SPACE-TIMER REMATERIALISED THERE ... MMM ... 21 MINUTES AND 40 SECONDS AGO. IT'S GOT TO BE XOMBUL.

NO TIME TO LOSE, THEN. I HAVE TO FIND HIM.

YES, ESPECIALLY AS OUR MAN AT THE 11TH-CENTURY RELAY DIDN'T SOUND VERY AWAKE. YOU CAN GO AND PICK UP YOUR ORDERS AT THE SPACEPORT'S SPATIO-TEMPORAL RELAY. YOU'RE SCHEDULED TO DEPART IN ... MMM ... EXACTLY 9 MINUTES. GOOD LUCK, VALERIAN. AND BE WARY OF XOMBUL. HE'S A FIRST CIRCLE TECHNOCRAT LIKE ME. HE'S SMART AND DANGEROUS ... AND PERHAPS INSANE, TOO!

THANKS, SUPER-INTENDENT! IF I'M NOT BACK IN ... MMM ... LET'S SAY A CENTURY OR TWO, SEND A WITCH TO RESCUE ME!

...I THINK I'LL HAVE ONE OF YOUR SOOTHE-BUBBLES. THIS WHOLE BUSINESS HAS ME WORRIED. AND THOSE DREAMS... TERRIBLE! SIMPLY TERRIBLE!

A SHORT TIME LATER, AT THE SPATIO-TEMPORAL RELAY BAR...

HELLO, BOYS AND GIRLS!

HEY! IT'S VALERIAN!

WHERE HAVE YOU BEEN HIDING?

I WAS ON HOLIDAY ON ONE OF THE PLANETS OF THE ARCTURUS SYSTEM. I EVEN FOUND TIME TO CREATE 14TH-DECIMAL MATHEMATICAL SCULP-TURES – I KID YOU NOT!

SHOW-OFF! I'M JUST BACK FROM A MISSION IN THE 22ND CENTURY – UNDER THE VEGETARIAN DYNASTY...

...SIX MONTHS OF SPINACH AND CRESS – CAN YOU IMAGINE? I HAVE A LOT OF CATCHING UP TO DO! WANT SOMETHING TO DRINK?

JUST A HYPER-PROTEIN COCKTAIL. I'M OFF ON A MISSION.

HEY, TRAN-LU... WHAT'S NEW WITH YOU?

MEH. A MISSION ON VENUS. THE USUAL STUFF: THE VENUSIANS HAD TURNED THE TERRAN COLONY'S TECHNOCRATS INTO POISONOUS MUSHROOMS – AGAIN. THEY DO LOVE THEIR PRACTICAL JOKES...

SOUNDS A LOT MORE PEACEFUL THAN MY LAST JOB! I HAD A WHOLE REGIMENT OF MUSKETEERS AFTER ME – COULDN'T EVEN TAKE THE TIME TO CHANGE BEFORE LEAVING BLASTED 18TH-CENTURY FRANCE!...

HA! HA! HA!

AGENT VALERIAN IS REQUIRED TO STOP AT HIS FIRST COCKTAIL!

...SINCE HE ONLY HAS 50 SECONDS LEFT TO GET TO HIS CRAFT AND REMATERIALISE AT THE AD 1000 RELAY! HOW YOU CAN WORK FOR THE SPATIO-TEMPORAL SERVICE AND STILL MANAGE TO BE LATE ALL THE TIME IS BEYOND ME...

FINE, FINE, I'M GOING!

HA!HA!

HA!HA!

HERE ARE YOUR ORDERS. OUR AGENT IN THE 11TH CENTURY, WESTERN EUROPE SECTION IS NAMED GEOFFROY, AND THE RELAY IS LOCATED INSIDE AN INN. THE CRAFT'S BEEN SERVICED AND YOUR COORDINATES LOCKED IN. GOOD LUCK!

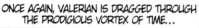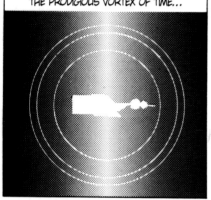

ONCE AGAIN, VALERIAN IS DRAGGED THROUGH THE PRODIGIOUS VORTEX OF TIME...

...AND INSTANTLY, 18 CENTURIES EARLIER...

WELL, THAT'S THE SPACE-TIMER XOMBUL USED... I'M ON THE RIGHT TRACK!

LET'S SEE THESE ORDERS. HMM... ITEM 12... ITEM 13... AH, HERE WE GO: THE SPATIO-TEMPORAL AGENT IS REMINDED THAT ONLY WEAPONS FROM THE CURRENT TIME PERIOD ARE ALLOWED, IN ORDER TO AVOID ANY TECHNOLOGICAL INTERFERENCE FROM MORE ADVANCED TIMES. NOTHING NEW HERE...

ITEM 15: PERIOD-APPROPRIATE CLOTHING IS AVAILABLE TO THE AGENT, AS WELL AS ALL THE NECESSARY EQUIPMENT FOR INSTANT MNEMONIC ACQUISITION OF THE 11TH-CENTURY VERNACULAR... RIGHT. NO TIME TO LOSE, THEN.

I'M TURNING INTO QUITE THE POLYGLOT. THESE MNEMONIC HELMETS REALLY ARE THE BEE'S KNEES.

XOMBUL MUST HAVE HAD VERY SPECIFIC REASONS TO COME HERE. HE MUST BE ON HIS GUARD... SO NOW THAT I SPEAK PERFECT OLD FRENCH AND AM PROPERLY ATTIRED... OH, WAIT, I STILL HAVE TO TRY ON THE HAT!

OOPS!!!... HATLESS IT IS, THEN!

WARNING
NOW ENTERING THE 11TH CENTURY

ONWARDS...

BEYOND THE HEAVY REINFORCED DOOR, THE MIDDLE AGES.

SPATIO-TEMPORAL RELAYS ARE WELL HIDDEN AS A MATTER OF COURSE ... BUT THEY WENT THE EXTRA MILE WITH THIS ONE!!!

HO! ANOTHER ONE... WHO ARE YOU?!

VALERIAN... I'M A TRAVELLER FROM THE CELLARS. AND YOUR NAME IS GEOFFROY, ISN'T IT?! WHAT HAPPENED?

OH, ARE YOU NOW? I'M GETTING A MITE SUSPICIOUS, YOU SEE! THE MISCREANT WHO ARRIVED BEFORE YOU NIGH ON BRAINED ME WITH A STOOL WHEN I ASKED HIM WHO HE WAS!...

...I DON'T WISH TO BE DRAGGED INTO YOUR BUSINESS. I'M PAID IN GOOD GOLD TO MAKE THE STRANGERS WHO COME UP FROM THE GREAT CELLAR SIGN HERE... NOTHING MORE – I HAVE NO INTEREST IN YOUR DEVILRY!...

WELL, I'M DONE... PREPARE SOME FOOD AND A FAST HORSE FOR ME. DO YOU KNOW WHERE XOMBUL ... ER ... THAT MAN WENT, BY ANY CHANCE?

WEST, TOWARDS ARELAUNE FOREST... NOW THIS WILL COVER THE MOUNT AND THE FOOD – BARELY. BUT AT LEAST YOU PAY IN GOOD COINS. THAT OTHER ONE, NOT ONLY DID HE CLOCK ME OVER THE HEAD...

...BUT HE ALSO STOLE A HORSE AND TWO LOVELY FAT ROAST CHICKENS!...

STOP YOUR WHINING. YOU PAID YOURSELF FROM MY PURSE – GENEROUSLY!

FAREWELL, FRIEND-LY INNKEEPER!

PAH! ONCE UPON A TIME, WE HAD IT EASY IN OUR CENTURY ... ASIDE FROM WOLVES, RATS, WITCHES AND THE OCCASIONAL RAIN OF FROGS. I WAS MAD TO CONSORT WITH THEIR KIND FOR A HANDFUL OF GOLD... NEVER AGAIN!

A FINE HORSE! FRIEND GEOFFROY DID WELL, ACTUALLY. I MUST BE GETTING CLOSE TO THE FOREST BY NOW. HOPEFULLY THOSE HARVESTERS CAN TELL ME...

HO, GOOD FOLKS! HAVE YOU PERCHANCE SEEN A RIDER HEADING TOWARDS THE FOREST?

YES, MY LORD. HE PASSED THROUGH THIS VERY PLACE!

BY ALL THE SAINTS IN HEAVEN! HE RODE LIKE THE DEVIL HIMSELF WAS ON HIS HEELS!

I SUPPOSE I SHOULD KEEP AFTER HIM, THEN.

WATCH YOURSELF, MY LORD! THOSE WOODS ARE CURSED. THAT RIDER MADE A GRAVE MISTAKE HEADING THERE. HEED MY WORDS, MY LORD, AND DON'T FOLLOW HIM!

THANK YOU FOR YOUR ADVICE, MY GOOD MAN, BUT I MUST PRESS ON.

THE DAY IS ALMOST DONE. YOU'RE RISKING YOUR LIFE – AND PERHAPS YOUR SOUL...

SOON THE EDGE OF THE FOREST APPEARS...

OH, RATS! I NEED TO CATCH UP WITH HIM BEFORE NIGHT-FALL, OR I MIGHT LOSE HIS TRAIL ENTIRELY...

THE TREES BECOME INCREASINGLY HUGE...

...THE PATH IS MORE AND MORE DIFFICULT TO TREAD...

THE PEASANTS WEREN'T KIDDING. THIS FOREST IS REALLY STRANGE.

...AND OMINOUS ENCOUNTERS SOON ABOUND.

WHOAH, CALM DOWN! KEEP GOING!!! DON'T TELL ME YOU'RE STARTING TO BELIEVE IN WITCHCRAFT TOO?!!

THERE'S NO WAY TO FOLLOW XOMBUL'S TRAIL IN THE DARK, ANYWAY. WE MIGHT AS WELL STOP AND SPEND THE NIGHT HERE!

THESE ENORMOUS LEAVES ARE WEIRD ... BUT AT LEAST THEY CAN MAKE A PERFECT BED!

EVERYTHING IS SO CLOSED-IN AND GLOOMY... WHAT COULD HAVE DRIVEN XOMBUL, HEAD OF 2720'S DREAMS DEPARTMENT, TO COME TO SUCH A TIME PERIOD?... IF ONLY I COULD HAVE BROUGHT MY PORTABLE RADAR TO FOLLOW HIM... OH WELL. GOTTA FOLLOW REGULATIONS...

ALL RIGHT... GOODNIGHT, HORSEY!

THE NEXT DAY AT DAWN...

TRAPPED! THE LEAF CURLED IN ON ITSELF AS I SLEPT ... AND THE EDGES ARE AS SHARP AS STEEL! WHAT AM I SUPPOSED TO DO?

I THINK YOU FELL FOR ONE OF THE FOREST'S TRAPS, STRANGER...

?

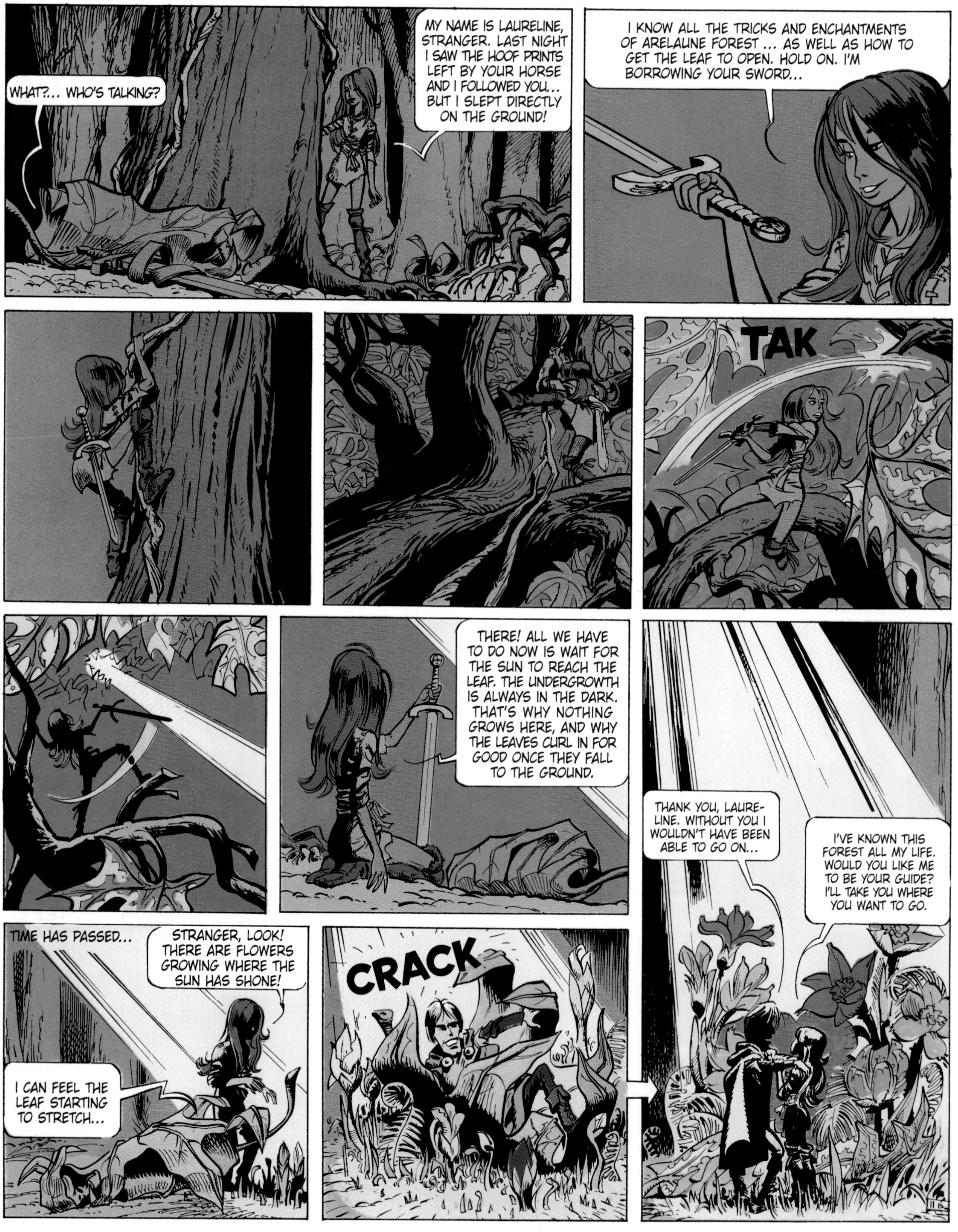
WHAT?... WHO'S TALKING?
MY NAME IS LAURELINE, STRANGER. LAST NIGHT I SAW THE HOOF PRINTS LEFT BY YOUR HORSE AND I FOLLOWED YOU... BUT I SLEPT DIRECTLY ON THE GROUND!
I KNOW ALL THE TRICKS AND ENCHANTMENTS OF ARELAUNE FOREST ... AS WELL AS HOW TO GET THE LEAF TO OPEN. HOLD ON. I'M BORROWING YOUR SWORD...
TAK
THERE! ALL WE HAVE TO DO NOW IS WAIT FOR THE SUN TO REACH THE LEAF. THE UNDERGROWTH IS ALWAYS IN THE DARK. THAT'S WHY NOTHING GROWS HERE, AND WHY THE LEAVES CURL IN FOR GOOD ONCE THEY FALL TO THE GROUND.
TIME HAS PASSED...
STRANGER, LOOK! THERE ARE FLOWERS GROWING WHERE THE SUN HAS SHONE!
I CAN FEEL THE LEAF STARTING TO STRETCH...
CRACK
THANK YOU, LAURE-LINE. WITHOUT YOU I WOULDN'T HAVE BEEN ABLE TO GO ON...
I'VE KNOWN THIS FOREST ALL MY LIFE. WOULD YOU LIKE ME TO BE YOUR GUIDE? I'LL TAKE YOU WHERE YOU WANT TO GO.

I WAS PURSUING ANOTHER RIDER, BUT I'M AFRAID I LOST HIS TRAIL DURING THE NIGHT!

IF YOU TAKE ME ON YOUR BEAUTIFUL HORSE, I WILL LEAD YOU TO SOMEONE WHO CAN HELP.

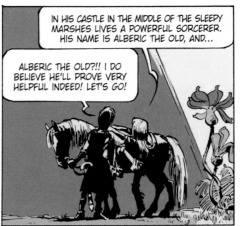

IN HIS CASTLE IN THE MIDDLE OF THE SLEEPY MARSHES LIVES A POWERFUL SORCERER. HIS NAME IS ALBERIC THE OLD, AND...

ALBERIC THE OLD?!! I DO BELIEVE HE'LL PROVE VERY HELPFUL INDEED! LET'S GO!

LATER...

...AFTER A LONG RIDE THROUGH A LANDSCAPE SCOURED BY THE POISONOUS WINDS BLOWING FROM THE MARSHES...

BREATHING THAT MIST WOULD PUT US TO SLEEP, YOU SAID, SO WE'LL CUT LONG REEDS AND USE THEM TO DRAW IN AIR FROM ABOVE IT.

I THINK I HAVE AN IDEA.

HERE'S THE RAFT. BUT THERE'S A LOT OF MIST TODAY...

AND SOON...

33

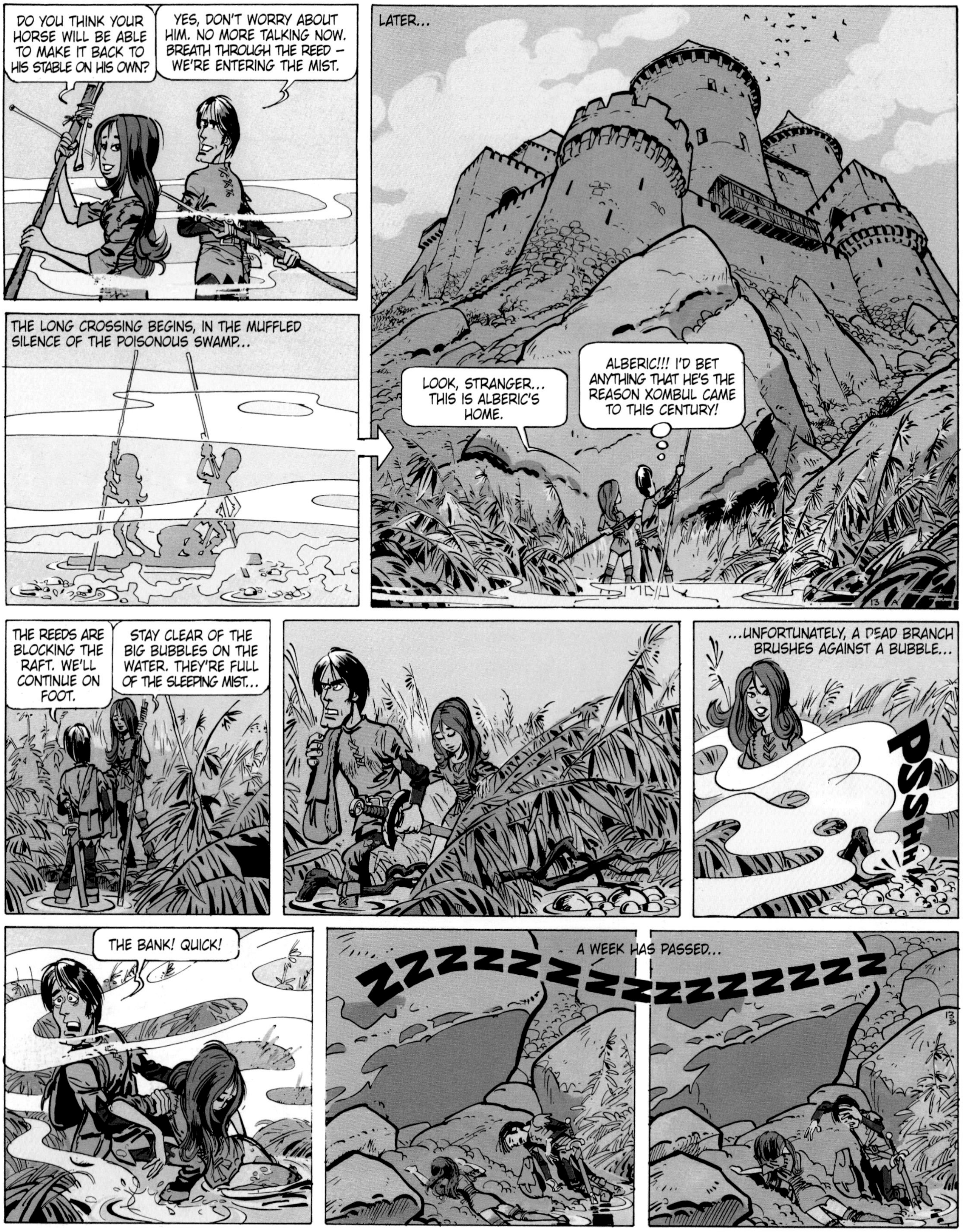
DO YOU THINK YOUR HORSE WILL BE ABLE TO MAKE IT BACK TO HIS STABLE ON HIS OWN?
YES, DON'T WORRY ABOUT HIM. NO MORE TALKING NOW. BREATH THROUGH THE REED – WE'RE ENTERING THE MIST.
THE LONG CROSSING BEGINS, IN THE MUFFLED SILENCE OF THE POISONOUS SWAMP...
LATER...
LOOK, STRANGER... THIS IS ALBERIC'S HOME.
ALBERIC!!! I'D BET ANYTHING THAT HE'S THE REASON XOMBUL CAME TO THIS CENTURY!
THE REEDS ARE BLOCKING THE RAFT. WE'LL CONTINUE ON FOOT.
STAY CLEAR OF THE BIG BUBBLES ON THE WATER. THEY'RE FULL OF THE SLEEPING MIST...
...UNFORTUNATELY, A DEAD BRANCH BRUSHES AGAINST A BUBBLE...
PSSHH
THE BANK! QUICK!
A WEEK HAS PASSED...
ZZZZZZZZZZZZZZZZZZZZ

MMM... I SLEPT WELL!

SO DID I ... BUT I WONDER FOR HOW LONG...

COME ON. I HAVE TO SEE ALBERIC RIGHT AWAY!

HUH! THIS COULD PROVE EVEN HARDER THAN I THOUGHT. THAT HULKING FELLOW DOESN'T LOOK FRIENDLY... TIME TO GET SNEAKY!

YIKES! SO MUCH FOR SNEAKING! HE'S ABOUT TO CHARGE US!

!?

CRACK

CRACK

HEY, THIS MIGHT BE OUR CHANCE!!!

READY?!

ARR GROO!

?

BOM

NOW LET'S GET IN BEFORE THAT MONSTER RAISES THE ALARM.

EVERYTHING SEEMS QUIET, BUT THAT DOESN'T MEAN MUCH. THERE COULD BE OTHER GUARDIANS...

GOODNESS... AREN'T YOU AFRAID, STRANGER?

PSHHH! WE CAN'T GO BACK NOW, ANYWAY. I NEED TO KNOW WHAT'S GOING ON INSIDE THIS CASTLE. COME ON...

SHEESH! THIS IS A REAL MAZE!!! WELL, LET'S KEEP GOING AND LEAVE IT TO CHANCE...

IF WE TRY THE DIFFERENT PATHS, WE'RE BOUND TO FIND SOMEONE OR SOMETHING EVENTUALLY.

THERE, THAT PASSAGEWAY...

YES. LET'S TAKE A LOOK.

AARGROOO

AAAAH!!! THERE'S SOMEONE ALL RIGHT! RUN LAURELINE!

GRRRRR

HA

CLICK

LAURELINE!

CLONC

!

SAFE! COME AND GET ME NOW, YOU BIG OAF!

?

BUT EVEN AS VALERIAN BEGINS CLIMBING, USING EVERY AVAILABLE NOTCH IN THE WALL, A HEAVY MECHANISM IS TRIGGERED...

CLICK

...AND THE WALL ROTATES...

YOU'VE LOST, YOUNG PUP!!

?

XOMBUL!

THAT'S RIGHT, MY DEAR VALERIAN. YOU'VE LOST! I KNEW THE OLD GOAT WOULD CHOOSE YOU FOR A SENSITIVE MISSION SUCH AS THIS, SO I WAS WAITING FOR YOU. I WAS SORT OF HOPING YOU WOULDN'T MAKE IT TO THE CASTLE, BUT KNOWING YOUR SKILLS, I PREPARED THIS QUAINT LITTLE WELCOME PARTY ANYWAY...

LET ME WARN YOU RIGHT NOW: DO NOT ATTEMPT SOMETHING THAT COULD COST YOU DEARLY! THESE CREATURES WOULD MAKE KINDLING OUT OF YOU IN THE BLINK OF AN EYE. FOLLOW ME, MY YOUNG FRIEND, AND GET READY TO GAZE UPON SOME MIRACLES.

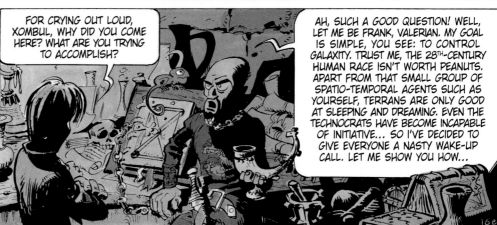

FOR CRYING OUT LOUD, XOMBUL, WHY DID YOU COME HERE? WHAT ARE YOU TRYING TO ACCOMPLISH?

AH, SUCH A GOOD QUESTION! WELL, LET ME BE FRANK, VALERIAN. MY GOAL IS SIMPLE, YOU SEE: TO CONTROL GALAXITY. TRUST ME, THE 28TH-CENTURY HUMAN RACE ISN'T WORTH PEANUTS. APART FROM THAT SMALL GROUP OF SPATIO-TEMPORAL AGENTS SUCH AS YOURSELF, TERRANS ARE ONLY GOOD AT SLEEPING AND DREAMING. EVEN THE TECHNOCRATS HAVE BECOME INCAPABLE OF INITIATIVE... SO I'VE DECIDED TO GIVE EVERYONE A NASTY WAKE-UP CALL. LET ME SHOW YOU HOW...

DISRUPTING THE DREAMS WASN'T ENOUGH. WHAT I NEEDED TO SHAKE GALAXY OUT OF ITS APATHY WERE TRUE NIGHTMARISH FIGURES – CREATURES OF FLESH AND BLOOD STRAIGHT OUT OF OUR ANCESTORS' BAD DREAMS. WHILE DOING SOME RESEARCH AT THE CENTRAL LIBRARY, I FOUND A MANUSCRIPT THAT MENTIONED ALBERIC. A FIRST-CLASS SORCERER, BELIEVE ME...

OH, THAT'S THE MANUSCRIPT I READ AT YOUR PLACE.

1000 ANNO DOMINI! A TIME MADE FOR ME! WHEN I GOT HERE, IT WAS CHILD'S PLAY TO ABUSE ALBERIC'S TRUST. HE'S TOO NAIVE, REALLY...

NAIVE, BUT ALSO THE KEEPER OF EXTRAORDINARY SECRETS! NOW, I, XOMBUL, CAN TRANSFORM PEOPLE AS I PLEASE, TURN THEM INTO CREATURES THAT OBEY ME BLINDLY. I'M GOING TO TAKE MY FIRST TROOPS BACK TO GALAXY USING THE RELAY'S SPATIO-TEMPORAL TRANSPORTER, AND LET THEM SPREAD CHAOS...

AFTER THAT, BY SIMPLY CHANTING THE SACRAMENTAL INCANTATION I WILL MAKE A SLAVE OUT OF ANY HUMAN I WANT. I'LL HAVE ALL THE POWER THEN, AND I WILL LEAD EARTH INTO A GLORIOUS AND RENEWING CRUSADE. I WILL REKINDLE **WAR!!!**

FOR A WHILE, I HOPED I COULD RECRUIT MEN OF ACTION SUCH AS YOU, BUT I CAN SEE THAT'S UNLIKELY...

...SO LET'S HEAD DOWNSTAIRS. I'LL SHOW YOU THE RESULTS OF MY WORK!

17A

ALLOW ME TO MAKE THE INTRODUCTIONS: THIS IS ALBERIC, THE GREATEST SORCERER OF THE TURN OF THE MILLENNIUM! HA! HA! HA! POOR OLD DEVIL! LOOK AT HIM NOW: HE'LL FOLLOW MY EVERY ORDER...

CROOCROOOOOOO CHEEP!

A GOOD THING I WAS PRECONDITIONED... WHAT A HORRIBLE SIGHT FOR A MAN OF GALAXY!!!

...HIS MANSERVANT. WHAT'S LEFT OF HIM, ANYWAY...

17B

...AND I HAVE A LITTLE SURPRISE FOR YOU...

LAURELINE!

THAT'S RIGHT, VALERIAN! EXPRESS ACCESS TO THE DUNGEONS IS AVAILABLE FROM THROUGHOUT THIS CASTLE... I'M GOING TO LET YOU WITNESS A TRANSFORMATION. THE SPELL IS DIFFICULT, AND I STILL GET IT WRONG NOW AND THEN, BUT THE RESULT SHOULD BE INTERESTING...

YOU MONSTER! I'M GOING TO...

POK

POK

THERE... QUICK AND EASY. I DID TELL YOU NOT TO MISBEHAVE... I'M PROBABLY TOO LENIENT WITH YOU, BUT ANYWAY. ENOUGH CHILDISHNESS – LET'S MOVE ON TO THE SPELL...

A UNICORN?!! GAAAAAAH! I SHOULD HAVE REMEMBERED THE MANUSCRIPT... YOU CAN'T TRANSFORM A PURE SOUL INTO JUST ANYTHING! AH, NEVER MIND. SHE'S COMING ANYWAY, ALONG WITH THE OTHERS!

YOU, PREPARE OUR DEPARTURE FOR GALAXITY AND BRING OUT THE PRISONERS. YOU, PUT THIS SPOILSPORT YOU KNOW WHERE...

AND A FEW HOURS LATER...

GOODBYE, VALERIAN! I'M AFRAID YOUR FRIENDS IN GALAXITY MIGHT WAIT A LONG TIME FOR YOUR RETURN...

WE SHOULD BE SOMEWHERE UNDERNEATH THE POOLS NOW. IT'S A GOOD THING THIS TUNNEL WAS HERE, BECAUSE GETTING ACROSS THE MARSHES WOULD HAVE BEEN IMPOSSIBLE WITH THESE CLUMSY FOOLS!

AFTER SOME DIFFICULT SLOGGING...

AHH! IT'S BEGINNING TO RISE – WE'RE FINALLY GOING TO GET OUT OF HERE! MOVE IT... MOVE IT...

WHAT'S GOING ON? OH, FOR GOODNESS' SAKE!!! THAT MORON IS STUCK!

GUARDS!
CLEAR THE WAY!

NO, NO! PUSH HIM! WE NEED TO GET OUT!!!

UNDER THE REPEATED BLOWS, WATER BEGINS TO SEEP OUT OF THE DAMP, ROTTING WALLS...

UNTIL SUDDENLY...

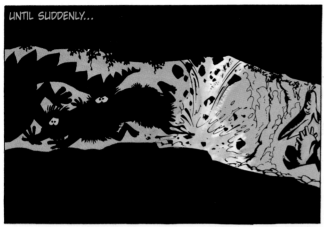

FORWARD TO THE EXIT! THE WHOLE GALLERY IS GOING TO FLOOD... *RUN* I SAID!

TAKING ADVANTAGE OF THE CONFUSION, LAURELINE SLIPS AWAY AND GALLOPS BACK TO THE CASTLE...

MEANWHILE...

WHEW... XOMBUL'S LITTLE FRIENDS ARE A BIT HEAVY-HANDED... I'VE GOT THE MOTHER OF ALL HEADACHES!

WELL, BLAST AND DOUBLE BLAST! LOCKED UP TIGHT... AND EVEN IF I HAD MY SWORD, WHAT GOOD WOULD IT DO ME IN HERE?... STILL, NO WAY I'M DYING INSIDE THIS THING...

IF ONLY I COULD USE SOME TOOL FROM THIS MESS...

NOT A TOOL – THAT!!!

41

AFTER A FEW UNSUCCESSFUL ATTEMPTS...

YES! **I GOT IT!**

I DON'T THINK THIS LOCK WILL WITHSTAND THE ACID VERY LONG...

RIGHT! NOW I NEED TO AVOID GETTING LOST IN THIS BOOBY-TRAPPED MAZE OF A CASTLE AGAIN. ONLY ONE WAY...

...THE WINDOW!

HELLO!

LAURELINE? IS THAT YOU?!? AND YOU CAN SPEAK??

UNICORNS CAN SPEAK, MY DEAR SIR!

HOW ON EARTH DID YOU ESCAPE?

OH, THAT WAS ACTUALLY EASY! BUT THE TUNNEL XOMBUL USED TO ESCAPE IS COMPLETELY FLOODED NOW.

LOOK! THE WATER LEVEL IN THE MARSH HAS LOWERED, AND THE SLEEPING MIST HAS ALMOST DISAPPEARED... WE SHOULD BE ABLE TO GO ACROSS!

HMM... FIRST I NEED TO FIND A HORSE IF I WANT ANY HOPE OF CATCHING XOMBUL BEFORE THE RELAY... LET ME GO TO THE STABLES.

NOW I'M PROPERLY EQUIPPED – THIS OLD SWORD COULD PROVE USEFUL!

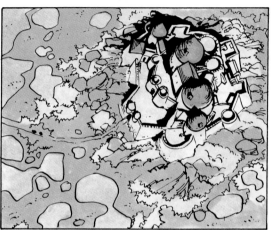

FIRST THE UNICORN ESCAPES, AND NOW THESE IDIOTS ARE ALREADY FALLING ASLEEP. WE'LL HAVE TO PITCH CAMP AND SET OFF AGAIN TOMORROW AT DAWN...

STOP HERE AND SLEEP TO YOUR HEART'S CONTENT. YOU NEED TO BE WELL RESTED FOR YOUR ARRIVAL IN 2720. HA! HA! HA! I CAN ALREADY PICTURE THE FACES OF THOSE GALAXY SLUGGARDS WHEN THEY SEE YOU! OH, THE GLORIOUS PANIC!!!

AFTER A LONG DETOUR THROUGH THE MARSHES...

AH! WE FOUND THEIR TRACKS AT LAST!... NIGHT WILL SOON BE HERE, BUT WE STAND A CHANCE OF CATCHING UP WITH THEM TOMORROW MORNING.

THE NEXT DAY AT DAWN...

HMM. I'LL NEVER BE ABLE TO ARREST XOMBUL WHILE HIS BODYGUARDS ARE THERE... BETTER FIND ANOTHER WAY...

THEY'LL HAVE TO GO THROUGH THE FOREST. COME ON, LAURELINE! WE'LL SET A TRAP FOR THEM THERE!

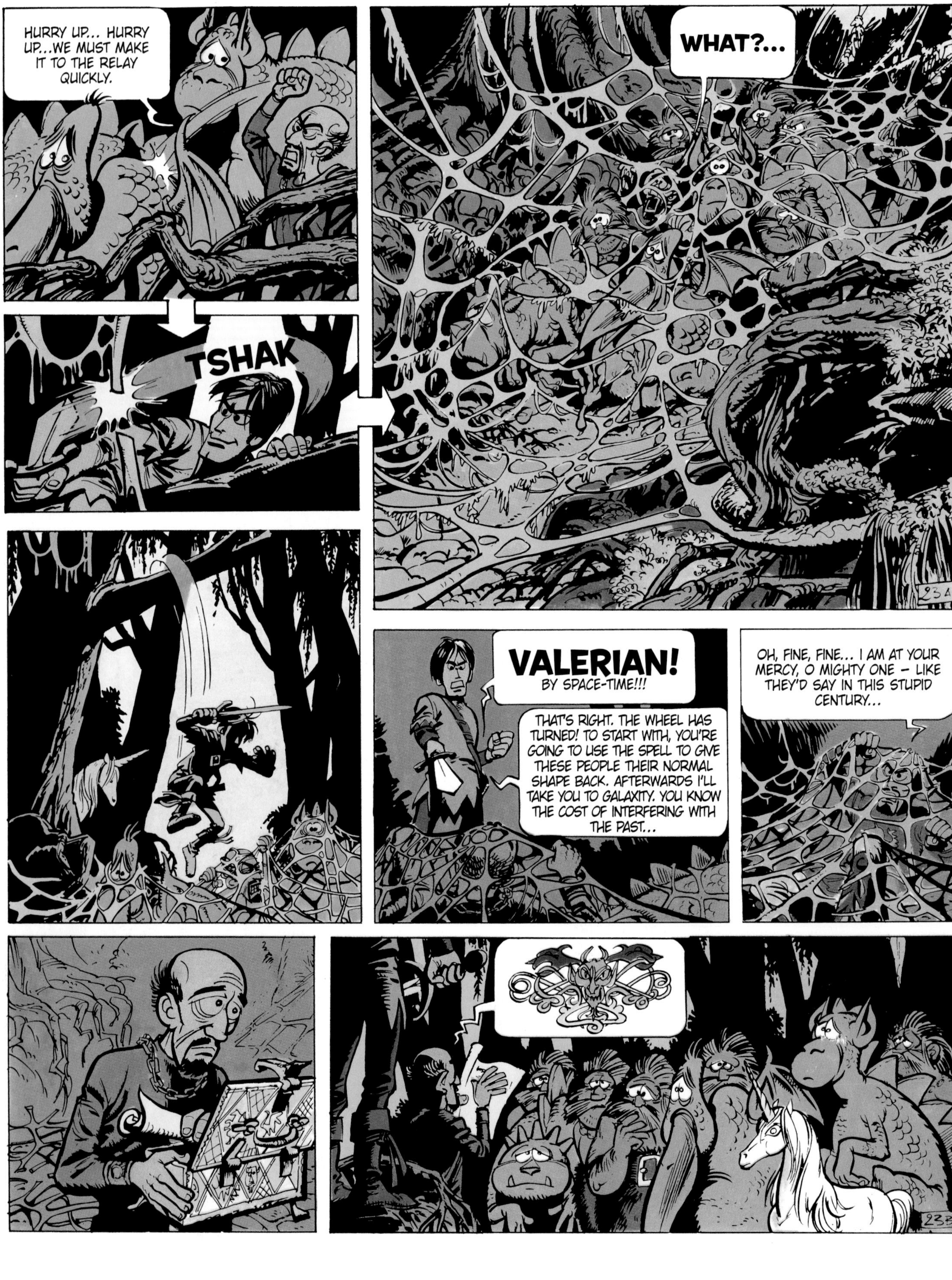
HURRY UP... HURRY UP...WE MUST MAKE IT TO THE RELAY QUICKLY.
TSHAK
WHAT?...
VALERIAN! BY SPACE-TIME!!!
THAT'S RIGHT. THE WHEEL HAS TURNED! TO START WITH, YOU'RE GOING TO USE THE SPELL TO GIVE THESE PEOPLE THEIR NORMAL SHAPE BACK. AFTERWARDS I'LL TAKE YOU TO GALAXITY. YOU KNOW THE COST OF INTERFERING WITH THE PAST...
OH, FINE, FINE... I AM AT YOUR MERCY, O MIGHTY ONE – LIKE THEY'D SAY IN THIS STUPID CENTURY...
23A
23B

LAURELINE! IT'S WONDERFUL!!!

OH, IT WASN'T THAT BAD, REALLY... YOU LEARN THINGS WHEN YOU'RE A UNICORN...

AAAAH! THAT'S NICE!

HA! HA! YOU WERE SO UGLY, MATE!

YES! I FEEL SO MUCH BETTER IN MY OWN SKIN!

LIKE YOU LOOKED ANY BETTER!

THAT SCALLYWAG XOMBUL TOOK ME BY SURPRISE, BUT I'M GOING TO SHOW HIM WHAT MY OWN MAGIC CAN DO! LET ME TURN HIM INTO A CANE TOAD!

LOOK OUT! XOMBUL IS STILL READING HIS MAGIC WORDS!!!

RATS! HE'S TURNED HIMSELF INTO A HAWK! HE'LL MAKE A BEELINE FOR THE SPATIO-TEMPORAL RELAY – WITH THE SCROLL!

I HAVE TO GO AFTER HIM! GOOD-BYE, LAURELINE... NO ONE MUST FOLLOW ME WHERE I'M GOING...

WHY NOT?... DID YOU KNOW THAT UNICORNS CAN READ MINDS? YOU COME FROM ANOTHER TIME, SOMEWHERE IN THE FUTURE. AND NOW THAT I KNOW YOUR SECRET, YOU DON'T HAVE ANY CHOICE BUT TO TAKE ME WITH YOU, RIGHT?!

BY THE GREAT NEBULA!!! I'VE INTERFERED WITH THE PAST AS WELL... AND TIME IS FLYING... TELL ME, ALBERIC, COULD YOU PROVIDE ME WITH A HORSE FOR LAURELINE?

THAT'S EASY, MY YOUNG FRIEND. I DON'T NEED TO MUMBLE OVER A SCROLL LIKE THAT NEOPHYTE...

IT'S NICE TO BE ON TWO LEGS AGAIN, ISN'T IT?

CERTAINLY IS...

HERE! TAKE THIS RING. IT'S A TALISMAN AGAINST THE SPELL. IT CAN'T FAIL, BUT IF THAT ROGUE THREATENS YOU, DON'T DO WHAT I DID AND FORGET TO USE IT AT THE RIGHT TIME...

COUNT ON ME. THAT SORCERER'S APPRENTICE IS GOING TO PAY FOR HIS CRIMES. LET'S GO, LAURELINE.

AND SO THE TWO RESUME RIDING THROUGH THE FOREST...

...WHILE IN THE AIR...

A LITTLE LATER...

OW! OW! OW! OW!

WHAT ABOUT ME? I HOPE MY GOOD MASTER ALBERIC ISN'T GOING TO KEEP ME AS A HORSE FOR TOO LONG!...

DID YOU SEE SOMETHING OR SOMEONE?

I SAW NOTHING – BUT I DEFINITELY FELT...

...SOME SORT OF NASTY BIRD, ALL SHARP CLAWS AND BEAK... I GRABBED MY BROOM AND WENT TO GIVE IT A GOOD WALLOP WHEN POOF! A DEVIL APPEARED, SMELLING LIKE BRIMSTONE, AND THEN...

TO THE RELAY! WE MIGHT STILL HAVE A CHANCE OF CATCHING XOMBUL...

...AND THEN... HO! WAIT! WHAT ABOUT MY LITTLE SIGNATURE!?!

FOLLOW ME, LAURELINE – AND DON'T WORRY ABOUT WHAT YOU'LL SEE. AFTER ALL, A FORMER UNICORN SHOULD BE ACCUSTOMED TO WONDERS...

46

CAREFUL! HE MIGHT STILL BE IN THERE!
TOO LATE! XOMBUL'S ALREADY GONE. WELL, LAURELINE, YOU ARE NOW A FEW STEPS AWAY FROM THE 28TH CENTURY, AND THIS IS MY SPACE-TIMER... BY SIRIUS!!!
XB 27
ALL THE COMPUTER'S CIRCUITS ARE FRIED!!! XOMBUL SCRAMBLED THE ENTIRE PROGRAMING!!! I'LL HAVE TO DOUBLE-CHECK EVERYTHING!
26A
ALL THESE LIGHTS ARE QUITE PRETTY! WHAT DO THEY DO?
LISTEN, YOU SHOULD USE THE MNEMONIC MACHINE WHILE I CARRY OUT REPAIRS. IT'LL TEACH YOU EVERYTHING YOU NEED TO KNOW... AND PUT ON A TRAVEL SUIT, TOO...
TIME PASSES...
LAURELINE, CAN YOU CHECK IF THE MCPHERSON INDUCTION LAW IS REACTING?
OK, ON IT!
AT LAST...
THERE, ALL DONE. NEVERTHELESS, XOMBUL'S SABOTAGE WAS A MASTER-STROKE. WE'RE GOING TO TRAVEL EIGHTEEN CENTURIES, BUT STILL WE'LL ARRIVE IN GALAXITY THREE AND A HALF DAYS AFTER HIM...
AND SO, ONCE MORE...
26B

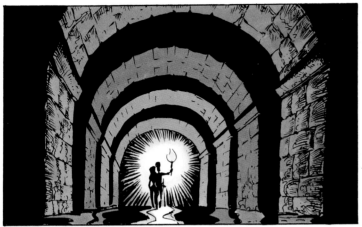

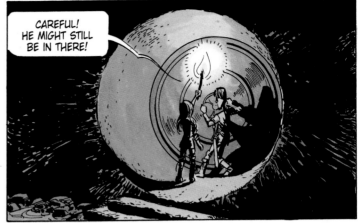

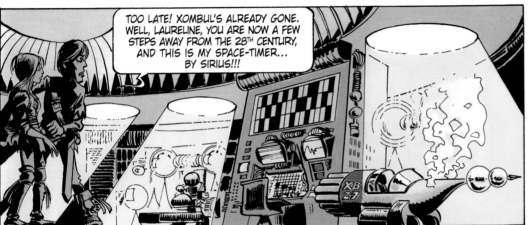

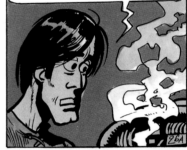

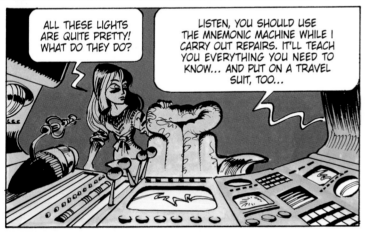

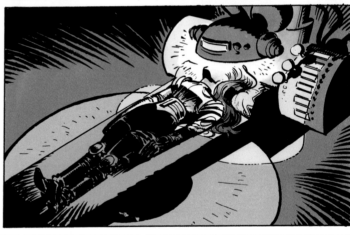

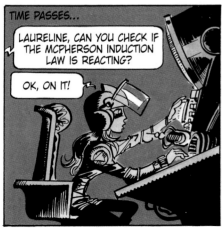

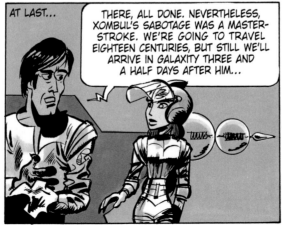

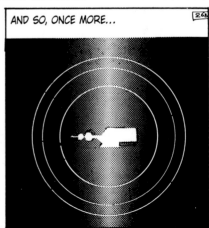

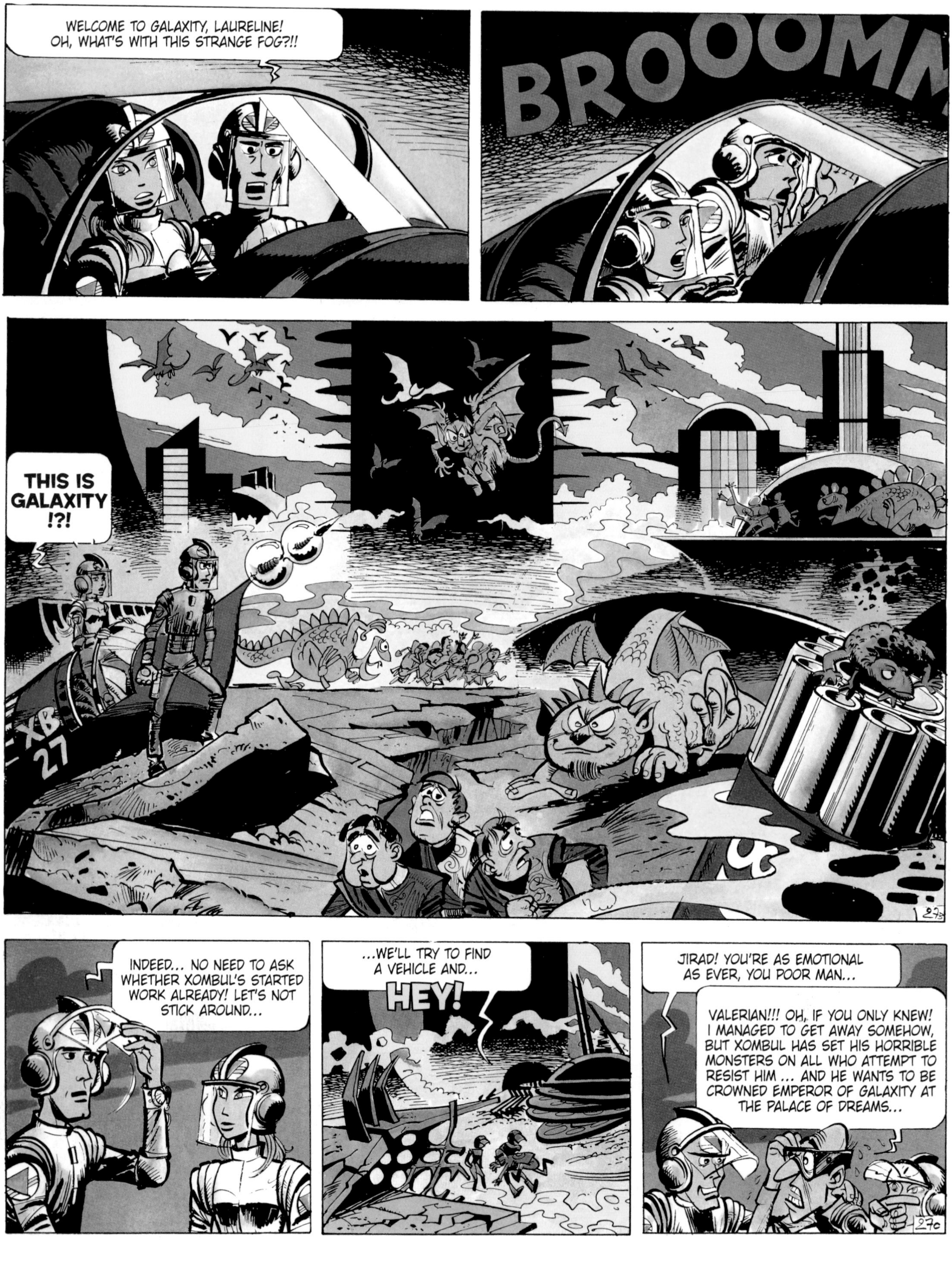
WELCOME TO GALAXITY, LAURELINE! OH, WHAT'S WITH THIS STRANGE FOG?!!
BROOOMM
THIS IS GALAXITY !?!
INDEED... NO NEED TO ASK WHETHER XOMBUL'S STARTED WORK ALREADY! LET'S NOT STICK AROUND...
...WE'LL TRY TO FIND A VEHICLE AND...
HEY!
JIRAD! YOU'RE AS EMOTIONAL AS EVER, YOU POOR MAN...
VALERIAN!!! OH, IF YOU ONLY KNEW! I MANAGED TO GET AWAY SOMEHOW, BUT XOMBUL HAS SET HIS HORRIBLE MONSTERS ON ALL WHO ATTEMPT TO RESIST HIM ... AND HE WANTS TO BE CROWNED EMPEROR OF GALAXITY AT THE PALACE OF DREAMS...

EMPEROR OF GALAXITY!!! BY THE GREAT NEBULA, HE'S INSANE!!! QUICKLY, D'YOU KNOW HOW WE CAN GET TO THE PALACE?

ER... THERE MIGHT STILL BE SOME SERVICEABLE BUBBLES UNDER THE DEBRIS...

EVERYTHING'S IN RUINS! WHAT HAPPENED?

AFTER ENCHANTING ALL HIS ENEMIES, XOMBUL AIMED THE DREAM MACHINES AT THE CITY TO MAKE THE PANIC COMPLETE... AS FOR THE SUPERINTENDENT, HE'S BEEN CAPTURED, BUT NO ONE KNOWS WHERE HE'S BEING KEPT...

SEE THE MACHINES THERE, ON TOP OF THE TOWERS...

VALERIAN! A FLYING DRAGON IS ATTACKING!

XOMBUL IS UP TO HIS OLD TRICKS – USING HIS MONSTERS TO GUARD HIS APPROACHES. WE'RE GOING TO HAVE TO DO SOME FANCY MANOEUVRING. HOLD ON TIGHT!

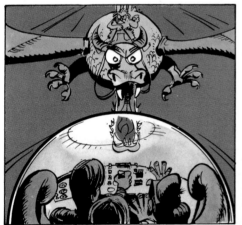

CLAP

WELL, FORTUNATELY XOMBUL'S CREATURES AREN'T EXACTLY THE SHARPEST TOOLS IN THE SHED. I HOPE WE'RE NOT LATE FOR THE CROWNING CEREMONY...

IT'S SO EMPTY... EVERYONE MUST BE GATHERED IN THE GREAT COMPUTER ROOM FOR THE CROWNING...

OK, JIRAD, GO AND SHUT DOWN THE DREAM MACHINES. I'LL TAKE CARE OF XOMBUL!

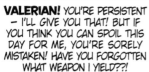

?!

AND SO I NOW CROWN MYSELF XOMBUL I, FIRST EMPEROR OF GALAXITY!!

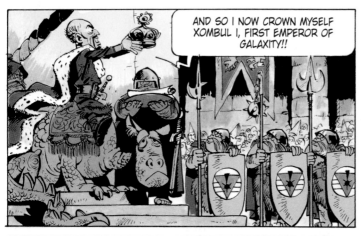

VERY GOOD, XOMBUL! SPLENDIDLY EXTRAVAGANT, VERY IMPRESSIVE! BUT THOSE WERE THE LAST HISTORIC WORDS OF YOUR REIGN, I'M AFRAID...

VALERIAN! YOU'RE PERSISTENT – I'LL GIVE YOU THAT! BUT IF YOU THINK YOU CAN SPOIL THIS DAY FOR ME, YOU'RE SORELY MISTAKEN! HAVE YOU FORGOTTEN WHAT WEAPON I YIELD??!

I'VE GOT A WEAPON TOO, XOMBUL!

...IF OLD ALBERIC'S TALISMAN DOESN'T WORK, I'M GOING TO LOOK VERY SILLY...

XOMBUL, YOUR REAL PROBLEMS ARE ABOUT TO BEGIN!

AT THE SAME INSTANT, JIRAD FINISHES DISCONNECTING THE DREAM MACHINES, AND THE COMPUTER ROOM'S APPEARANCE RETURNS TO NORMAL...

ALL RIGHT, XOMBUL, SINCE YOU SEEM TO HAVE A TASTE FOR NIGHTMARISH CREATURES...

...THEN I THINK YOUR PUNISHMENT IS SELF-EVIDENT! VALERIAN, GIVE ME THAT SPELL...

GOOD IDEA, SUPERINTENDENT. AND SINCE XOMBUL IS A BIT OF AN ODD BIRD IN GALAXITY...

...LET'S PUT HIM SOMEWHERE HE CAN HAVE SOME QUIET TIME TO REFLECT...

A LITTLE LATER...

GALAXITY IS SO BEAUTIFUL!

YES, IT WAS ALL JUST A BAD DREAM – WASN'T IT, JIRAD?

HMM! STILL, WE SAW SUCH HORRORS...

UGH. I WAS EVEN STARTING TO GET USED TO WALKING ON FOUR LEGS... JIRAD, GIVE ME ONE OF YOUR SOOTHE-BUBBLES – I NEED IT...

THE END

SCRIPT LINUS.

THE CITY OF SHIFTING WATERS

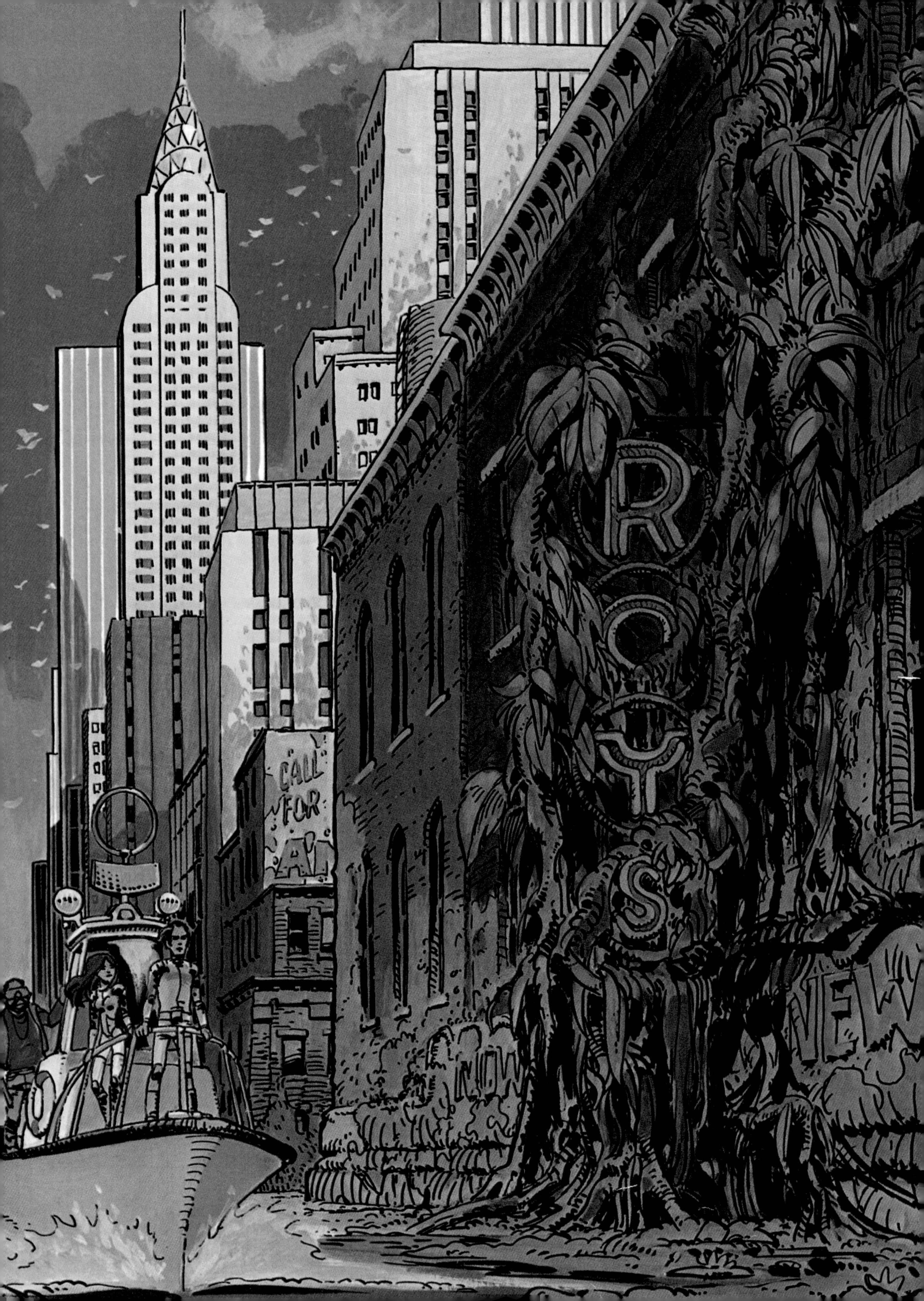
CALL FOR
NOW
NEW

GALAXITY, METROPOLIS OF THE FUTURE AND CAPITAL OF THE TERRAN GALACTIC EMPIRE. WITH THE DEVELOPMENT OF INSTANT SPACE-TIME TRAVEL, THE STRUCTURE OF SOCIETY HAS CHANGED. THE AGE OF LEISURE HAS COME FOR GOOD; BUT THE SPATIO-TEMPORAL AGENTS SERVICE—TO WHICH VALERIAN AND LAURELINE BELONG—IS IN CONSTANT ACTIVITY. THE AGENTS' MISSION IS TO PATROL BOTH HISTORY AND THE UNIVERSE TO SAFEGUARD EARTH AND ITS EMPIRE. FOR NOW, THE TWO YOUNG AGENTS ARE ON HOLIDAY AFTER A PARTICULARLY SENSITIVE MISSION IN THE HYDROPONIC FARMS OF VENUS. A GAME OF 3D CHESS IS RAGING; THE COMPUTERS ARE WORKING AT FULL CAPACITY...

AND CHECK, VALERIAN!

WHOA, THERE, LAURELINE. YOU HAVEN'T WON YET!... JUST A FEW CALCULATIONS TO MAKE AND YOU'LL SEE...

DING DING

AGENT VALERIAN, REPORT TO THE OFFICE OF THE SUPERINTENDENT OF THE SPATIO-TEMPORAL SERVICE... AGENT VALERIAN, REPORT TO...

OH, WELL... GOT TO GO...

HMM... YOU'RE NOT USUALLY IN SUCH A HURRY TO GO SEE THE BOSS... YOU SORE LOSER!

A SHORT WHILE LATER, SPATIO-TEMPORAL SERVICE OFFICES...

WELL, YOU MADE GOOD TIME FOR ONCE! I MUST SAY, YOUR ASSISTANT'S HAVING A GOOD INFLUENCE ON YOU, VALERIAN...

SO, WHAT'S GOING ON, SIR?

GALAXITY'S ONLY POLITICAL PRISONER, THE DANGEROUS XOMBUL, HAS ESCAPED. THAT MADMAN WHO WANTED TO DISLOCATE OUR SOCIETY TO BECOME ITS DICTATOR IS NOW FREE. THE WORST THING IS THAT HE GOT HIS HANDS ON ONE OF OUR SPATIO-TEMPORAL SHIPS AND IS MOVING AROUND HISTORY FREELY. IF HE GETS IT INTO HIS HEAD TO MODIFY OUR PAST, OUR CIVILISATION'S VERY EXISTENCE IS UNCERTAIN...

BY THE GREAT NEBULA! WHERE AND WHEN DID HE REMATERIALISE?

WELL, THAT'S THE STRANGEST THING. HE SHOWED UP IN NEW YORK IN 1986... AND YOU'RE GOING TO FOLLOW HIM THERE...

YOU MUST BE KIDDING, SIR!

WHAT'S SO WEIRD ABOUT THAT?

LET ME EXPLAIN, MY YOUNG FRIEND. I SEE YOU DON'T KNOW EVERYTHING ABOUT GALAXITY'S HISTORY YET. ACTUALLY, NO ONE KNOWS EXACTLY WHAT HAPPENED IN OUR PAST BETWEEN 1986 AND THE 24TH CENTURY. IT'S A MYSTERIOUS ERA: THE DARK AGES OF THE EARTH. THAT WAS WHEN TRADITIONAL CIVILISATION WAS SWEPT AWAY BY A CATACLYSM...

HERE, LOOK AT THESE PICTURES: THEY WERE TAKEN FROM ONE OF THE PRIMITIVE SATELLITES THAT USED TO ORBIT THE EARTH BACK THEN. THEY'RE THE ONLY DOCUMENTS WE HAVE—AND THEY WERE DAMAGED BY RADIATION...

IN 1986, A HYDROGEN BOMB DEPOT LOCATED NEAR THE NORTH POLE ACCIDENTALLY BLEW UP. HERE YOU CAN SEE A SNAPSHOT OF THE EXPLOSION. THE ICECAPS IMMEDIATELY BEGAN TO MELT... THE CLIMATE BECAME MUCH HOTTER ALL ACROSS THE GLOBE, AND THE SEA LEVEL ROSE BY SEVERAL DOZEN FEET, SWALLOWING MOST LARGE CITIES...

EVERYTHING HAPPENED VERY QUICKLY! TWO WEEKS LATER, THE VERY SHAPE OF THE CONTINENTS HAD CHANGED BEYOND RECOGNITION. NATIONS HAD BROKEN UP; SCIENTIFIC ARCHIVES HAD BEEN LOST FOREVER...

WASN'T IT DURING THOSE CURSED YEARS THAT SPACE-TIME TRAVEL WAS INVENTED— EVENTUALLY ALLOWING EARTH TO REBUILD ITS POWER?

SO IT IS SAID, VALERIAN, ALTHOUGH THE FIRST ACTUAL MACHINE DATES BACK TO 2314. BUT THE TIME IN BETWEEN IS SHROUDED IN COMPLETE SECRECY, SINCE THE CHARTER DRAFTED BY GALAXITY FORBIDS ALL TRAVEL TO THAT ERA. I'VE BEEN THINKING, THOUGH. THE SITUATION IS TOO SERIOUS: WE HAVE TO DISOBEY THE CHARTER... THEREFORE, I'M ASKING YOU TO GO AND SEARCH FOR XOMBUL...

BUT... SIR, THE ZONE IS FORBIDDEN; WE DON'T EVEN KNOW WHAT SHAPE THE RELAYS ARE IN! WHAT'LL HAPPEN IF MY SPACE-TIMER MATERIALISES UNDER 200 FEET OF WATER?

IT'S A RISK YOU'LL HAVE TO TAKE! SINCE THE AUTOMATIC SYSTEMS NOTIFIED US OF XOMBUL'S ARRIVAL, IT MEANS THAT THE RELAY'S STILL WORKING. YOU HAVE MY FULL CONFIDENCE! YOU'RE LEAVING IMMEDIATELY. I'M KEEPING LAURELINE HERE—IF NEEDED, SHE CAN GO INTO ACTION ONCE WE RECEIVE THE FIRST MESSAGE FROM YOU...

IF YOU EVER RECEIVE ONE!... OH, WELL, DON'T WORRY—I CAN SWIM...

BE CAREFUL, VALERIAN...

AND AFTER SOME QUICK PREPARATIONS, IN AN INSTANT VALERIAN'S SPACE-TIMER CROSSES THE CENTURIES SEPARATING GALAXITY FROM...

... NEW YORK, 1986!

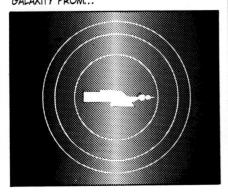

WELL, THE RELAY'S NOT QUITE A FISH TANK YET, BUT IT'S WELL ON ITS WAY TO BECOMING ONE! I'D BETTER GET OUT OF HERE QUICK...

EVERYTHING IS ROTTEN FROM THE DAMP. AND I WONDER WHERE THAT MUFFLED THUMPING IS COMING FROM...

!?!
OH, THAT'S GREAT! BRILLIANT CHOICE FOR THE RELAY'S LOCATION! HOW AM I GOING TO MAKE MY WAY OUT? I'D BETTER THINK HARD.

WHAT...?
THE STATUE IS COLLAPSING!

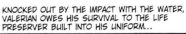

KNOCKED OUT BY THE IMPACT WITH THE WATER, VALERIAN OWES HIS SURVIVAL TO THE LIFE PRESERVER BUILT INTO HIS UNIFORM...

AND MUCH LATER...

HEY...

LOOK OVER THERE!... THERE'S A GUY IN THE DRINK... MIGHT BE ONE OF OURS. HEAD FOR HIM...

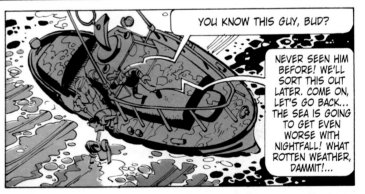

YOU KNOW THIS GUY, BUD?

NEVER SEEN HIM BEFORE! WE'LL SORT THIS OUT LATER. COME ON, LET'S GO BACK... THE SEA IS GOING TO GET EVEN WORSE WITH NIGHTFALL! WHAT ROTTEN WEATHER, DAMMIT!...

IS HE ALIVE AT LEAST?

YEAH, BUT HE'S OUT COLD...

57

IN THE FLOODED STREETS OF NEW YORK, THE LAUNCH SLOWLY THREADS ITS WAY THROUGH THE UNHEALTHFUL VEGETATION THAT FLOURISHES IN THE SWELTERING HEAT...

ALFONSO, YOU TIE HIM UP AND LEAVE HIM IN THE TWELFTH-FLOOR STOREROOM... WE'LL TAKE CARE OF HIM LATER! WE'RE LEAVING IN TWO MINUTES TO FINISH THE WORK...

OK, BUD, WE'LL BE RIGHT BACK!

5A

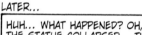

LATER...

HUH... WHAT HAPPENED? OH, YEAH... THE STATUE COLLAPSED... THE DIVE... AND NOW I'M ALL TRUSSED UP IN HERE...

MUST BE THE FOOD SECTION IN A DEPARTMENT STORE... EVERYTHING LOOKS TRASHED!

WHOEVER IT WAS THAT DUMPED ME INSIDE THIS RATHOLE, I HAVE TO GET OUT...

JUST A LITTLE PATIENCE... THIS WILL DO...

A FEW MINUTES LATER...

THERE, THAT'S DONE! AND IT SOUNDS LIKE IT WAS JUST IN TIME—I'M ABOUT TO HAVE GUESTS...

5B

SO! WE CAN HAVE A LITTLE CHAT WITH OUR FLOATING SURVIVOR AT LAST...

WITH ANY LUCK, I'LL FIND OUT WHAT THIS IS ALL ABOUT...

HEY, NUTS: ALFONSO TOLD YOU THAT'S WHERE HE'D LEFT THE GUY, RIGHT?... SO WHERE IS HE???

WHAT?! YOU DON'T REMEMBER?!! MAN, YOU'RE LOSING IT COMPLETELY, NUTS!... I'M WARNING YOU...

FORGET IT, BUD! IF WE WANT TO FINISH CLEANING UP THE FIFTH AVENUE JEWELLERS TODAY, WE'D BETTER GET A MOVE ON!

GOT IT... THESE CLOWNS ARE RANSACKING THE CITY! NOTHING TO DO WITH XOMBUL...

... I'M OUT OF HERE! HEY!

WHOA! LOOK AT THE STRANGE RATS YOU FIND AROUND HERE!!!

LET'S GET HIM!!!

ANOTHER FLOOR OR TWO AND I SHOULD BE AT WATER LEVEL. PERHAPS I'LL MANAGE TO SHAKE THEM OFF!

MOMENTS LATER AND A FEW FLOORS DOWN...

BUD! I SAW SOMETHING PASS BY THE WINDOW... HE MUST HAVE DIVED!

WHERE THE HELL DID THAT GUY GO?

THERE! THAT'S HIM!

LET'S GET THE LAUNCH!!

TWO FLOORS UP...

THEY BOUGHT IT! NO NEED TO THROW ANOTHER DUMMY... ESPECIALLY A BRIDE... AND NOW, LET'S VAMOOSE!

DAMN! A DUMMY IN A WEDDING TUX!

WE'VE BEEN HAD!

NO! LOOK OVER THERE!

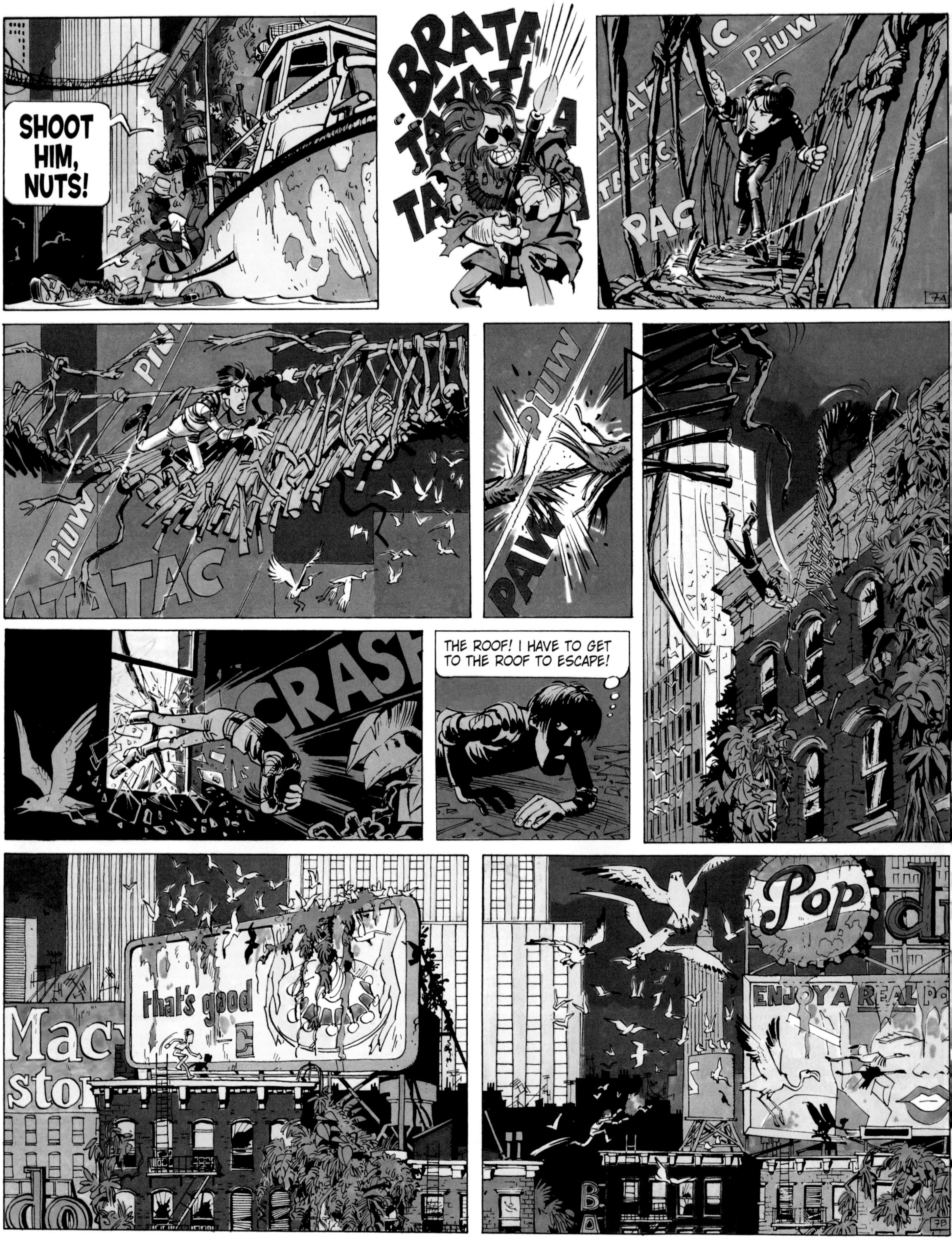
SHOOT HIM, NUTS!
BRATA
TAC
PiUW
PAC
PiUW
PiUW
TAC
PiUW
THE ROOF! I HAVE TO GET TO THE ROOF TO ESCAPE!
that's good
Pop
ENJOY A REAL

VALERIAN SLOWLY MAKES HIS WAY THROUGH THE JUNGLE THAT COVERS THE ROOFTOPS OF THE OLD BUILDINGS, UNTIL...

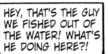

HEY, THAT'S THE GUY WE FISHED OUT OF THE WATER! WHAT'S HE DOING HERE?!

HEY, STOP!

NOT SO FAST, PALS—YOU DON'T HAVE ME JUST YET!

8A

A LITTLE WHILE LATER...

WELL! I MADE IT THROUGH TODAY, BUT TALK ABOUT A WELCOMING COMMITTEE! AND NONE OF THIS HELPED ME GET ANY CLOSER TO XOMBUL. THE CITY LOOKS COMPLETELY DESERTED, MY WOULD-BE RESCUERS ASIDE... EVEN THE EMPIRE STATE BUILDING IS DEAD. HEY... THAT'S THE TALLEST BUILDING IN MIDTOWN MANHATTAN... THIS GIVES ME AN IDEA...

I LOST MY GUN!! BUT WE'RE NOT DONE, YOU AND ME!

ALFONSO, WE'D BETTER GO GET SOME REINFORCEMENTS...

8B

THIS CITY'S GOING TO GIVE ME A HEART ATTACK... 1797 STEPS... THAT'S TOUGH, EVEN FOR AN AGENT OF SPACE-TIME...

STILL, IF ANYTHING'S GOING ON SOMEWHERE IN THIS AREA, HERE'S WHERE I HAVE THE BEST CHANCE OF FINDING OUT...

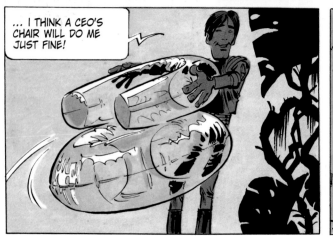

PITCH BLACK... LET'S SEE OVER THIS WAY!...

HEY! A LIGHT!

INTERESTING!... THERE'S A LIGHT ON THE TOP FLOOR OF THE UNITED NATIONS BUILDING!... AND YET THERE'S NO POWER IN NEW YORK! THIS ISN'T THE STYLE OF MY EARLIER GANGSTERS. NOTHING TO LOSE BY GOING THERE TO HAVE A CLOSER LOOK!

GREAT, MORE STEPS... BUT NO WAY I'M SWIMMING TO THE UN; I NEED SOME KIND OF RAFT!...

AND AFTER SOME TIME SPENT SEARCHING FRUITLESSLY...

HO HO! THE BOARD MEMBERS HAD QUITE A COMFY SETUP HERE!...

... I THINK A CEO'S CHAIR WILL DO ME JUST FINE!

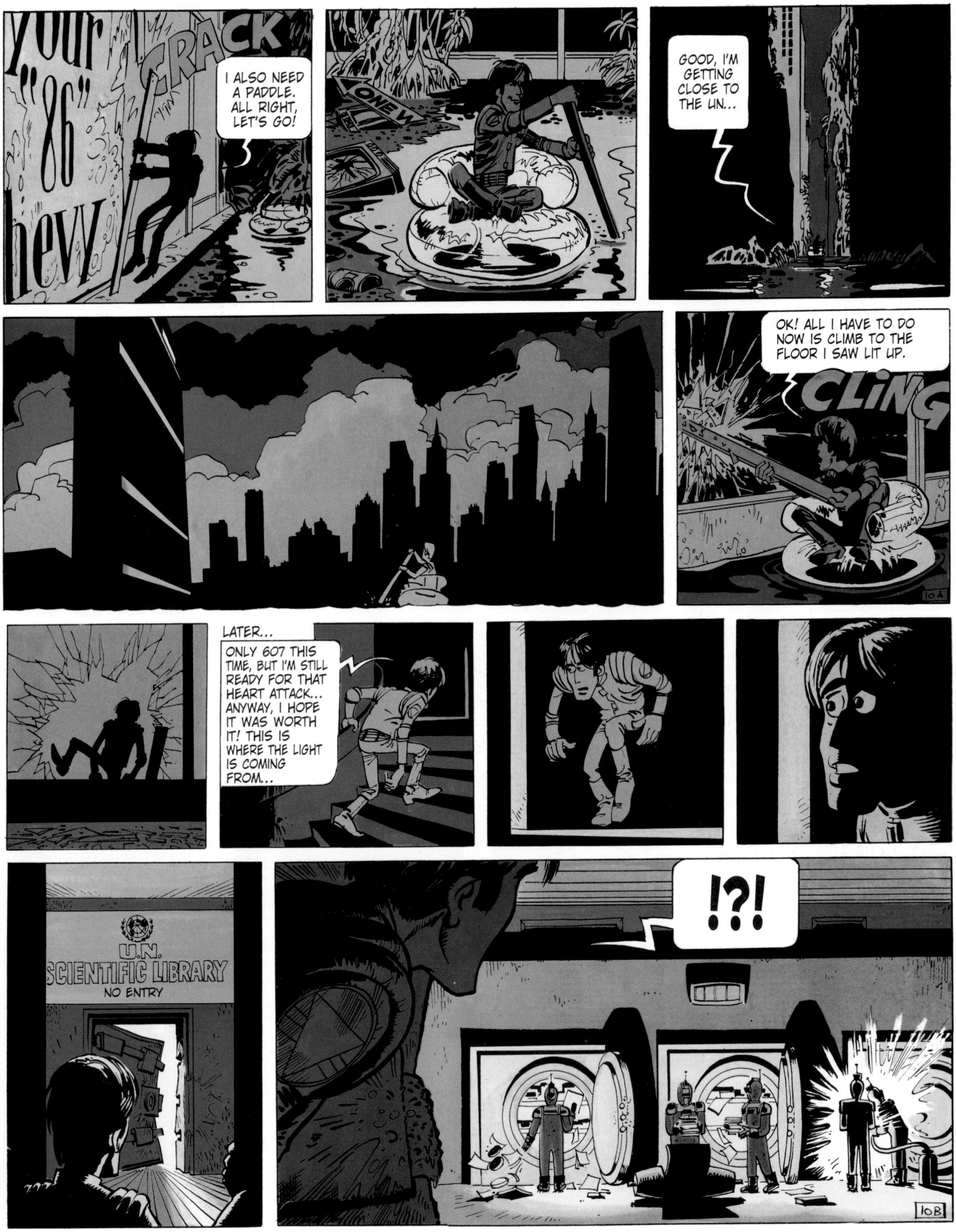
your "86" hevy
CRACK
I ALSO NEED A PADDLE. ALL RIGHT, LET'S GO!
ONE W
GOOD, I'M GETTING CLOSE TO THE UN...
OK! ALL I HAVE TO DO NOW IS CLIMB TO THE FLOOR I SAW LIT UP.
CLING
10A
LATER...
ONLY 607 THIS TIME, BUT I'M STILL READY FOR THAT HEART ATTACK... ANYWAY, I HOPE IT WAS WORTH IT! THIS IS WHERE THE LIGHT IS COMING FROM...
U.N.
SCIENTIFIC LIBRARY
NO ENTRY
!?!
10B

IT WAS DEFINITELY WORTH IT! WHO ARE THESE WEIRDOES BUSY PILLAGING SCIENTIFIC ARCHIVES!?!... BY BETELGEUSE!... THEY'RE...

THEY'RE ROBOTS!

AND SOON...

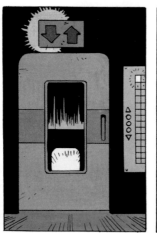

GROUND FLOOR!... THE ELEVATOR IS BELOW SEA LEVEL!!!

ONLY ONE THING TO DO... FIND MYSELF SOME DIVING EQUIPMENT AND GO TO WHERE THE ELEVATOR STOPS! I DON'T KNOW IF XOMBUL IS BEHIND THIS, BUT IT LOOKS LIKE I HAVE AN INTERESTING LEAD!...

LATER...

HEY! LOOK WHO'S COMING! I'LL BE DAMNED!!!

WATCH THIS. THIS'LL BE A GOOD LAUGH!

POP

POP

HEY?

SHPAM

ALL RIGHT, GET IN! ENOUGH OF YOUR LITTLE NIGHTLY EXCURSIONS!... YOU AIN'T TOO SMART AFTER ALL...

I WAS PLANNING TO DO YOU IN; BUT SINCE WE'RE A BIT SHORT-HANDED, YOU'RE GOING TO MAKE YOURSELF USEFUL...

HA HA HA!!!

PLOP PLOP PLOP PLOP

SO, DID THE LOSERS FROM THE "AUTHORITIES IN EXILE" SEND YOU, THEN? YOU CAME TO SPY ON US, DIDN'T YOU? WELL, YOU'RE IN FOR A TREAT! OF COURSE, ONCE WE'RE DONE: BOOM... ONE TO THE HEAD. BUT UNTIL THEN, YOU'LL HAVE PLENTY TO SEE. DON'T YOU WORRY...

YOU KNOW, AS FAR AS I'M CONCERNED, YOU CAN GRAB ANYTHING YOU WANT! LET'S MAKE A DEAL: I LEAVE YOU ALONE, AND YOU DO THE SAME...

TSK TSK... SEE, WE'VE GOT OUR HANDS ON A NICE, FAT PILE OF LOOT! EVERY RICH CAT IN NEW YORK CITY RAN AT THE FIRST BIG WAVE—AND LEFT THEIR SAVINGS BEHIND... BELIEVE ME, THERE'S A LOT OF STUFF IN THE MUSEUMS, AND PLENTY OF CASH IN THE BANKS... SO, EVEN IF IT WASN'T THE COPS THAT SENT YOU, THERE'S NO WAY WE'RE GIVING YOU A CHANCE TO RAT ON US...

AS THE CRAFT KEEPS GOING UP FIFTH AVENUE TOWARDS CENTRAL PARK, THE SUN BEGINS TO RISE...

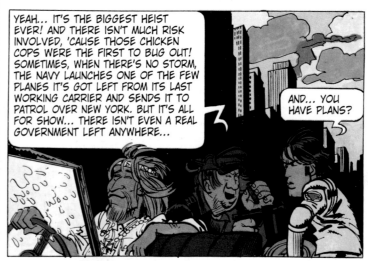

YEAH... IT'S THE BIGGEST HEIST EVER! AND THERE ISN'T MUCH RISK INVOLVED, 'CAUSE THOSE CHICKEN COPS WERE THE FIRST TO BUG OUT! SOMETIMES, WHEN THERE'S NO STORM, THE NAVY LAUNCHES ONE OF THE FEW PLANES IT'S GOT LEFT FROM ITS LAST WORKING CARRIER AND SENDS IT TO PATROL OVER NEW YORK. BUT IT'S ALL FOR SHOW... THERE ISN'T EVEN A REAL GOVERNMENT LEFT ANYWHERE...

AND... YOU HAVE PLANS?

SURE DO, BUDDY! ONCE THE HOLDS ARE FULL, THE BIG BOSS IS TAKING US WITH HIM. HE PROMISED US THE GOOD LIFE. AND BELIEVE ME, WHEN YOU SEE SUN RAE, YOU'LL UNDERSTAND WHY WE'RE WITH HIM...

12A

LOOK AT THAT! THE ONLY CARGO SHIP THAT DIDN'T SINK AT ITS MOORING WHEN THE WATER BEGAN TO RISE. WE SCROUNGED UP EVERY GALLON OF OIL LEFT IN NEW YORK. ANOTHER FEW DAYS TO FINISH LOADING UP AND WE'LL RAISE ANCHOR... AS RICH MEN! HA! HA! HA!

IT'S MORNING AT THE LOOTERS' HQ—THE GRAND PLAZA HOTEL...

THAT'S SUN RAE OVER THERE... YOU'D BETTER NOT DISTURB HIM WHILE HE'S PLAYING. HE'S MERCILESS WHEN THAT HAPPENS... NOW MOVE—YOU'RE GOING TO JOIN THE OTHER PRISONERS...

12B

THE DAYS GO BY, FILLED WITH EXHAUSTING LABOUR. THE HEAT IS MORE AND MORE OPPRESSIVE. STEADY RAIN STOPS ONLY FOR SUDDEN SQUALLS, AND THE WATER KEEPS RISING...

GET A MOVE ON, YOU LAZY BUMS. IT'S THE ROCKEFELLERS' SILVERWARE—SHOW SOME RESPECT, WILL YOU?

SEE THESE GOLD BRICKS? I GOT THEM FROM THE CHASE MANHATTAN BANK! IT'S NOT EASY TO CRACK A SAFE UNDER 10 FEET OF WATER!

... NO KIDDING! ME, I GOT ZIP. JUST A FEW HALF-ROTTED HUNDRED-DOLLAR BILLS...

HEY!

WHAT DO YOU THINK OF MY STATUE, EH? ME, I LIKE MUSEUMS BEST...

IT'S PRETTY, ISN'T IT?...

YOU SICK FOOL!... WE TOLD YOU BEFORE: WHAT'S IMPORTANT IS JEWELS... HE GETS CRAZIER ALL THE TIME, THAT GUY!...

ENOUGH TIME WASTED WITH YOUR CRAP... HEY! YOU OVER THERE... COME AND THROW THIS OVERBOARD...

PLOOF

THE AFTERNOON OF THE SAME DAY...

HO, DOWN THERE! ALL HANDS ON DECK! IT'S A STORM! THE SHIP'S BREAKING FROM ITS MOORING...

HMM! IT'S NOW OR NEVER!

... WHEN THE FIRST TS[...] STAYED THERE AND ARE [...] THEY CAN. THEIR WORS[...] NOW, ALL SCIENTIFIC AR[...] BEEN IRRETRIEVABLY LO[...] THEY'LL HAVE TO START [...]

WELL! RATS LEAVING THE SINKING SHIP?

AAAAH!... THAT FEELS GOOD!

THE ONLY ONES WHO [...] BE THE BRAINS, AND [...] THOSE WITH THE POWE[...] BEHIND THEM!!! AND T[...] THING THAT I'M SURE X[...] HIS THIRST FOR PO[...] DREAMS OF CHANG[...] HISTORY—HAS ALREA[...]

NO NEED TO ADVERTISE MY DEPARTURE... COME HERE, YOU!

HEY, THERE'S SOME-ONE IN HERE!

SERIOUSLY?! BY SATURN, ARE YOU THAT KEEN ON GOING BACK TO SLAVE LABOUR?... OH WELL. LET'S START BY CHANGING OUR CLOTHES— OUR UNIFORMS ARE A BIT TOO CONSPICUOUS!

THAT ONE'S SMALL BUT TOUGH!...

OK, VALERIAN, THAT'S ENOUGH FOR TODAY... BESIDES, YOU SEEM SOMEWHAT OFF YOUR GAME!!!

LAURELINE! WHAT ARE YOU DOING HERE?!?

NOW'S NOT THE TIME FOR QUESTIONS! FOLLOW ME—I HAVE A DINGHY WAITING!

SOON, THE RAFT IS FLOATING AWAY THROUGH THE AILING TREES OF CENTRAL PARK...

THE CHEEK OF T
CHICKS!!! YOU K
SERVICE SHOUL
MEN—YOU'RE A
WHAT ARE YOU

WHEN T
STARVATION O
BEEN TOLD THEY
FOR JUST ABO
OF SUGAR OR A

FROM THE TREE WE'LL BE ABLE TO SEE INSIDE...

AND THERE THEY ARE...

WHAT ARE THEY DOING?

WE'LL KNOW IN A MOMENT. WE HAVE TO GET INSIDE TO HEAR WHAT'S GOING ON!

CENTRAL LAB CALLING NEW YORK BASE... CENTRAL LAB CALLING NEW YORK BASE...

THIS IS CENTRAL LAB. HAVE YOU COMPLETED YOUR TASK IN THE UNITED NATIONS BUILDING?

MISSION ACCOMPLISHED, SIR!

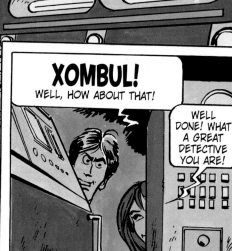

XOMBUL!
WELL, HOW ABOUT THAT!

WELL DONE! WHAT A GREAT DETECTIVE YOU ARE!

GOOD. THEN YOU WILL LEAVE IMMEDIATELY. WE'VE CALCULATED THAT THE LAST TSUNAMI WILL HIT NEW YORK CITY IN LESS THAN AN HOUR. THE REMNANTS OF THE ICECAP BROKE UP. BEFORE YOU DEPART, BLOW UP THE PLACE PER THE PLAN. I WANT NO TRACE OF YOUR EVER BEING THERE, UNDERSTOOD?

HEY, WHAT?...

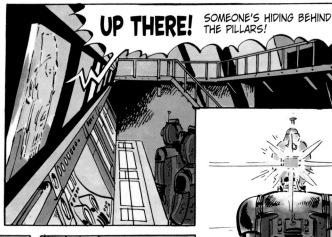

UP THERE! SOMEONE'S HIDING BEHIND THE PILLARS!

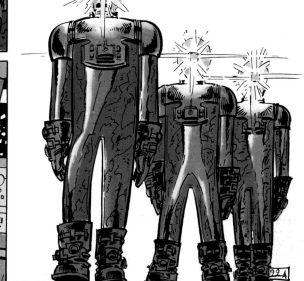

OK, TIME TO GO!

JUST WAIT A SECOND!

BAM

THIS IS THE CENTRAL LAB!
TURN ON ANOTHER SCREEN, YOU IMBECILES. I CAN'T SEE A THING!
HURRY UP!

THEY HAVE DISINTEGRATORS!

WE'VE GOT TO RUN!

NO! I'M STAYING! I'M NOT GOING TO LET THEM FRY US LIKE CHICKENS!

TAKE THEM ALIVE!

SAVE YOUR AMMO! THEY'RE IMPERVIOUS TO BULLETS!

I WANT THEM ALIVE! CAPTURE THEM! THEY CAN'T DO ANYTHING AGAINST YOU...

75

TRAPPED LIKE RATS! I CAN'T BELIEVE THIS!

SURRENDER!

NE PAKER

KNOWING THAT RESISTING WOULD BE POINTLESS, VALERIAN AND LAURELINE WALK TOWARDS THE SCREENS WHILE THE ROBOTS CARRY THE UNCONSCIOUS SUN RAE.

BY THE GALAXY!

IF IT ISN'T VALERIAN AND HIS INEVITABLE LITTLE GIRL!

HA HA HA!

... I DO SO LOVE THESE IMPROMPTU ENCOUNTERS! WELL, YOU'RE TOAST, VALERIAN. AND WHEN I SAY TOAST, I MEAN IN EVERY SENSE OF THE WORD... YOU'LL HAVE NOTICED WITH WHAT EASE MY... ER... ASSOCIATES CAN ROAST ANYTHING FROM AFAR... THEREFORE, I'D ADVISE YOU TO STAY PUT... BY THE WAY, WHO'S THAT BRUTE OF AN ACQUAINTANCE YOU HAVE NOW?

MY "ASSOCIATE," AS YOU PUT IT. BUT I HAVE BETTER TASTE THAN YOU IN THESE MATTERS: SUN RAE IS THE UNCONTESTED MASTER OF NEW YORK CITY, AND A FIRST-CLASS FLUTE PLAYER... WHEN HE'S NOT UNCONSCIOUS.

RIGHT... I SEE, ONE OF THE LOOTERS STILL ROAMING AROUND THE PLACE... WELL, YOU'RE ALL GOING TO JOIN ME HERE. UNDER CLOSE GUARD, BUT I DON'T WANT MY ASSOCIATES TO BE SEEN— THEY DO TEND TO STAND OUT, YOU SEE. SO, YOUR FLUTIST WILL PILOT THE HOVERCRAFT, SINCE HE KNOWS THE CITY SO WELL. OF COURSE, THERE WILL BE NO CONTACTING ANYONE. ONLY ONE ORDER: HEAD WEST. THE SLIGHTEST DEVIATION AND: PFFFIT... DISINTEGRATION, IS THAT CLEAR? NOW GO. **THE CATACLYSM COULD GET HERE ANY SECOND.** HAVE A NICE TRIP! I TRUST THAT YOU'LL MAKE IT OUT ALL RIGHT... YOU DON'T HAVE A CHOICE!

THEY'RE NOT EVEN WATCHING US!

OH, THEY DON'T NEED TO! THEY KNOW WE'RE STUCK WITH THEM NOW—THE HOVERCRAFT IS OUR ONLY CHANCE.

OK, ALL RIGHT! LET GO OF ME! SO, I GATHER THAT YOU'VE FOUND WHAT YOU WERE LOOKING FOR?

ER... IN A WAY, YES. THE TRIP WILL SERVE MY PURPOSE. OF COURSE, IT DOESN'T SOUND LIKE AS GOOD A DEAL FOR YOU.

YOU THINK SO?...

?

IS EVERYONE THIS DENSE ON WHATEVER PLANET YOU CAME FROM? I DON'T GIVE A DAMN ABOUT THAT BUNCH OF PUNKS PILING UP DOLLARS INSIDE A TUB THAT'S PROBABLY GOING TO SINK IN A FEW MINUTES. I THINK THERE'S A LOT MORE TO GAIN FROM THIS... HOW DO YOU CALL HIM... XOMBUL!

... IF I COULD UNDERSTAND WHAT MAKES HIS "ASSOCIATES" TICK, I THINK I COULD DO SOME FANCY WORK WITH A GANG LIKE THAT... COME ON, WE'RE BOARDING.

READY?!

THE CRAFT CROSSES THE SWAMP AT REDUCED SPEED...

INSIDE THE COCKPIT WHERE THEY'RE STAYING QUIETLY OUT OF SIGHT, ONE OF THE ROBOTS OBEYS XOMBUL'S COMMAND AND...

... REMOTELY TRIGGERS THE DESTRUCTION OF THE BUNKER, WHICH BLOWS UP WITH A THUN-DEROUS ROAR.

BOOM

AND THE POWERFUL MACHINE, ITS ENGINES RED-LINED, LEAPS FORWARD JUST ABOVE THE ROLLING WAVES, LASHED BY AN INCREASINGLY SAVAGE WIND...

UNDER THE SILENT BUT WATCHFUL SURVEILLANCE OF THE ROBOTS, IT'S ABOUT TO GO THROUGH NEW YORK CITY AND HEAD WEST...

A WATERSPOUT!

LOOK, OVER THERE!

INSIDE A NEW YORK CITY OPEN TO THE FURY OF THE ELEMENTS, A RACE AGAINST THE CLOCK BEGINS. IT IS RUN BY SUN RAE, WHOSE HERCULEAN STRENGTH AND KNOWLEDGE OF THE CITY SEEM TO MAKE A MOCKERY OF OBSTACLES.

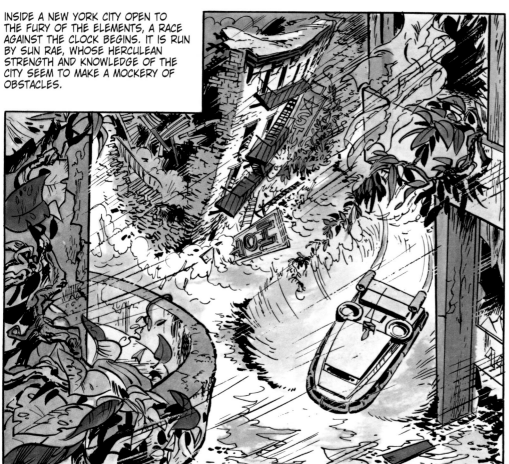

THIS THING HANDLES LIKE A DREAM!

PREFERRING TO AVOID THE FRAGILE, SHAKING HIGH-RISES, SUN RAE IS FORCED TO CHOOSE OPEN SPACES. THE MACHINE PLOUGHS THROUGH THE THICK CARPET OF ALGAE THAT PROLIFERATES ABOVE THE OLD PARKS...

BUT SUDDENLY...

DAMN! I CAN'T SEE A THING WITH ALL THIS CRAP ON THE WINDSHIELD!

WATCH OUT, SUN RAE!
THE WAVE IS HERE! ALL OF DOWNTOWN IS TUMBLING DOWN!

78

AND WHEN THE HOVERCRAFT ARRIVES NEAR THE BRIDGE...

UNDER THE TERRIFIC PRESSURE EXERTED BY THE TSUNAMI AS IT SWALLOWS THE CITY, THE POWERFUL STEEL CABLES OF THE SUSPENDED BRIDGE SNAP.

WITH A TERRIFYING CRASH, THE WHOLE STRUCTURE COLLAPSES INTO THE HUDSON RIVER. MIRACULOUSLY THE CRAFT, PUSHED BY THE WAVE, IS STILL AFLOAT. BUT...

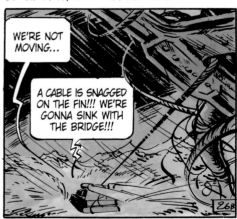

79

INEXORABLY, WASHINGTON BRIDGE SINKS BENEATH THE WAVES, PULLING THE TRAPPED HOVERCRAFT UNDER.

SUN RAE! REVERSE THE ENGINE! WE NEED TO GIVE THE CABLE SOME SLACK TO REMOVE IT!

IT'S WAY TOO HEAVY— WE'LL NEVER MOVE IT! WE'RE TOAST!!!

VALERIAN! LOOK OUT!!!

THE ROBOT, HAVING FREED THE CRAFT, WALKS TO THE CONTROLS, GUNS THE ENGINES AGAIN...

...AND, ALONG WITH THE REST OF HIS FELLOWS, HEADS DOWN BELOW AND OUT OF SIGHT.

WHERE ARE WE NOW?

IN THE SUBURBS. THE WORST IS OVER— THE TSUNAMI'S MOVED AWAY!

HEY! WHAT'S UP WITH THOSE CLOWNS? ARE THEY SEASICK OR SOMETHING?...

THEY MAY BE INVULNERABLE, BUT SPEED DOESN'T SEEM TO BE THEIR FORTE! AND APPARENTLY, THEY CAN ONLY COMMUNICATE ORALLY WITH XOMBUL...

WELL, HE COULD'VE HAD THEM ACT A BIT EARLIER! IT WOULD HAVE SPARED US AN AWFUL SCARE!...

HOURS GO BY. HAVING LEFT NEW YORK CITY FAR BEHIND, THE HOVERCRAFT TRAVELS ON THROUGH RUINED AREAS... EVERYWHERE, THE NOW-PASSED TSUNAMI HAS WREAKED HAVOC...

HELP!

STOP, PLEASE!

MURDERERS!! THEY'RE ABANDONING US!

THIS IS HORRIBLE, VALERIAN... ALL THOSE POOR PEOPLE.

YES, BUT WHAT CAN WE DO?... NOW THAT THE ROBOTS HAVE SWITCHED ON THE AUTOPILOT, WE DON'T EVEN KNOW WHERE WE'RE GOING...

LOOK AT WHAT'S LEFT OF CIVILI-SATION: A HALF-RUINED CAPITOL, AND ALL THESE BEAUTIFUL HOUSES TURNED INTO DESERTED ISLANDS...

YES, IT'S THE END OF A WORLD. AND WE'RE THE ONLY ONES TO KNOW THAT ANOTHER ONE WILL BE BORN OUT OF ALL THIS MISERY. OUR WORLD... GALAXITY'S WORLD...

THE HOVERCRAFT FORGES ON THROUGH THE CLAMMY AIR. STILL HEADING WEST, THE STRANGE CREW SAILS TOWARDS THE ROCKY MOUNTAINS, WHERE XOMBUL HAS ESTABLISHED HIS LAIR...

81

EARTH IN FLAMES

....

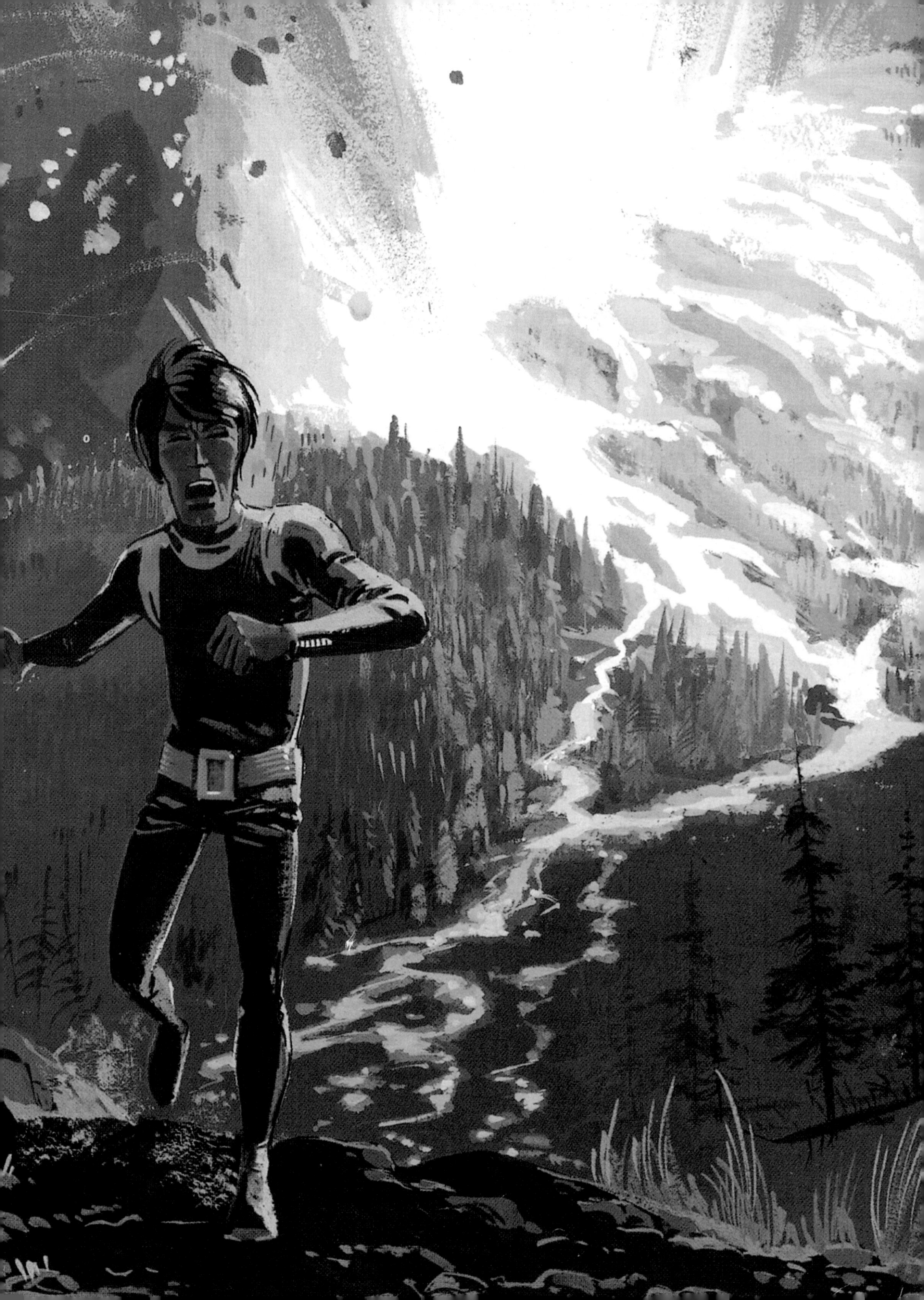

EVENTUALLY, A SWIFT CHANGE OF VEHICLE TAKES PLACE AT THE FOOT OF THE ROCKY MOUNTAINS, IN THE HEAVY ATMOSPHERE OF AN IMMINENT STORM. THE GROUP MADE UP OF VALERIAN, LAURELINE, SUN RAE AND XOMBUL'S CREATURES FINDS ITSELF INSIDE AN OLD ARMY HELICOPTER—AND READY TO FLY OVER THE FORBIDDING OBSTACLE...

THE HELICOPTER, PILOTED BY ONE OF THE ROBOTS, IS QUICKLY CAUGHT IN THE STORM...

UNDER THE CRASH OF LIGHTNING, IT THREADS ITS WAY BETWEEN ROCK WALLS...

... AT LAST, AFTER A DIFFICULT FLIGHT, IT MANAGES TO ESCAPE THE MOUNTAINS.

FUNNY, THIS LAND-SCAPE... I HAVE THE FEELING I'VE SEEN IT BEFORE!

ME, TOO! THIS GEYSER LOOKS FAMILIAR. UNLESS IT APPEARED AFTER THE DISASTER...

NO, NO... IT WAS THERE LONG BEFORE! WE'RE ABOVE YELLOWSTONE PARK, IN WYOMING! WHICH ALSO EXPLAINS THE BUFFALOS—IT'S THE LARGEST RESERVE OF WILD ANIMALS IN THE UNITED STATES...

THEIR TRIP COMPLETE, THE PASSENGERS HEAD INTO A CAVE. ONLY THREE OF THE ROBOTS STAY BEHIND AND BEGIN UNLOADING THE DOCUMENTS SNATCHED FROM NEW YORK CITY.

... THE JOURNEY CONTINUES UNTIL THE GROUP ARRIVES AT THE ENTRANCE TO A VAST LABORATORY.

INSIDE THE MOUNTAIN...

AH! THERE YOU ARE!

WELL, VALERIAN... WHO WOULD HAVE THOUGHT WE'D MEET AGAIN IN 1986! THE LAST TIME WE SAW EACH OTHER, WE WERE OLDER BY A FEW CENTURIES AND I WAS YOUR PRISONER.
A VERY UNPLEASANT SITUATION, YOU KNOW! FORTUNATELY, I STILL HAD A FEW ALLIES WHO LATER GOT ME OUT OF THAT PREDICAMENT...

THAT'S GOOD TO KNOW! I'LL HAVE TO TAKE CARE OF THEM WHEN I GET BACK!

OH, YOU KNOW, I'D BE SURPRISED IF YOU EVER WENT BACK TO WHERE YOU CAME FROM. BESIDES, I TOOK CARE TO DISPOSE OF THOSE COMPROMISING FRIENDS.

WHAT WAS ALL THAT JAZZ ABOUT?! I WISH I COULD UNDERSTAND...

FORGET IT! IT'S BUSINESS BETWEEN VALERIAN AND XOMBUL. AND IT'S A LITTLE COMPLICATED...

NO, NO... HE'S RIGHT! I DIDN'T BRING YOU HERE SO WE COULD DISCUSS THE PAST—OR MORE ACCURATELY, THE FUTURE. THE PRESENT IS MUCH TOO INTERESTING FOR THAT! COME, I'LL INTRODUCE YOU TO THE ONLY SCIENTIST WHO AGREED TO REMAIN WITH ME...

ALL THE OTHER SPECIALISTS OF THIS US ARMY SUPER-LABORATORY RAN LIKE RABBITS AS SOON AS THE CATACLYSM BEGAN. I ONLY MANAGED TO KEEP ONE, BUT I HAVE TO ADMIT HE'S REMARKABLE!

MR SCHROEDER...
MR SCHROEDER...

HE HATES BEING DISTURBED IN THE MIDDLE OF A DANGEROUS EXPERIMENT.

YES.. YES... WHAT NOW? I TOLD YOU BEFORE: JUST BECAUSE I'M YOUR PRISONER DOESN'T MEAN YOU SHOULD FEEL FREE TO PESTER ME EVERY FIVE MINUTES...

... I'M WILLING TO INVENT FOR YOU, BUT NOT CHITCHAT WITH YOU. UNDERSTOOD?... BESIDES, YOU HAVE NO CONVERSATIONAL SKILLS...

I SIMPLY WANTED TO INFORM YOU THAT THE DOCUMENTS FROM THE UNITED NATIONS HAD ARRIVED. AND... ER... MAY I ASK WHAT IMPORTANT EXPERIMENT YOU ARE CURRENTLY CONDUCTING?...

CAN'T YOU SEE? I'M MAKING SYNTHETIC WHISKY! WITH THE HORRIBLE SWILL YOUR ROBOTS COOK HERE...

... I NEED IT!

HA HA... OUR FRIEND SCHROEDER LOVES A GOOD JOKE!... BUT MAKE NO MISTAKE: HE'S UNDOUBTEDLY ONE OF THE MOST BRILLIANT SCIENTIFIC MINDS THAT EVER GRACED THE EARTH. AN ASSOCIATE WORTHY OF ME, IN TRUTH...

... AND YOU'VE ACTUALLY SEEN THE FIRST FRUITS OF OUR COLLABORATION: THESE ROBOTS THAT BROUGHT YOU HERE. STILL A BIT ROUGH, BUT ABSOLUTELY LOYAL. I SHOULD WARN YOU RIGHT AWAY THAT THEY ARE TUNED TO MY OWN BRAIN—AND OBEY ME ALONE...

ANYWAY, I DIDN'T BRING YOU HERE TO THREATEN YOU, SINCE YOU KNOW FULL WELL THAT YOU'RE TRAPPED. AS IT HAPPENS, I HAVE PLANS—AND I'M READY TO OFFER YOU A PART IN THEM. THE WORLD IS RIPE FOR ME TO GRAB AND SHAPE TO MY WILL. SCHROEDER IS PUTTING THE LAST TOUCHES TO SOME MILITARY EQUIPMENT WITH WHICH I INTEND TO IMPOSE MYSELF EASILY AS THE ONLY LEADER CAPABLE OF BRINGING THE EARTH OUT OF ANARCHY...

YOU, THE GANGSTER: I PROPOSE THAT YOU BECOME COMMANDER OF MY FUTURE TROOPS. AND YOU, VALERIAN, CAN BE MY RIGHT-HAND MAN FOR THIS COLOSSAL ENDEAVOUR. I'VE HAD THE OPPORTUNITY TO JUDGE YOUR SKILLS, BOTH OF YOU. WHAT DO YOU SAY?

HO HO... THIS SOUNDS INTERESTING...

YOU'VE GOT TO BE KIDDING!

YES, AMUSING... I'LL HAVE TO THINK ABOUT IT...

NO NEED! I HAD ANTICIPATED YOUR HESITATION, AND I THINK I HAVE A WAY TO HELP YOU THINK FAST. SO, PLEASE FOLLOW ME... WE'RE GOING TO CONDUCT A FUN, LITTLE APPLIED-PHYSICS EXPERIMENT ...

AT XOMBUL'S INVITATION, THE GROUP LEAVES THE LABORATORY AND HEADS DOWN INTO THE DEPTHS OF THE EARTH...

SUDDENLY, SCHROEDER PRETENDS TO TRIP...

YIKES! IT'S SLIPPERY HERE!!

... AND SLIPS A MYSTERIOUS OBJECT INTO VALERIAN'S HAND...

... TAKING ADVANTAGE OF THE CORRIDOR'S DARKNESS, HE WHISPERS HURRIEDLY...

THROW THIS DOWN WHEN I TELL YOU... WE MUST ESCAPE... I'M WITH YOU...

OH! SORRY...

... THEN, AS IF NOTHING HAD HAPPENED, THE TWO MEN WALK ON WITH THE OTHERS...

... AND COME TO A HUGE CAVE.

SEE THIS MACHINE HERE, VALERIAN?... THIS IS THE M.M.—THE FIRST MOLECULAR MINIATURISER!

SCHROEDER EVEN TESTED THE DEVICE BY SHRINKING A LIVE BUFFALO!!

LOOK AT IT. ISN'T IT CUTE? BUT THAT'S NOTHING! NEXT, I'M GOING TO TRY IT ON MAN—OR MORE ACCURATELY...

... WOMAN! YOUR FRIEND LAURELINE WILL BE MY FIRST TEST SUBJECT! YOU, TAKE HER TO THE PAD! SCHROEDER, TO YOUR CONSOLES.

DON'T WORRY, MISS! WE'RE JUST GOING TO MINIATURISE YOU NICELY. WE'LL HAVE TO DO IT IN SEVERAL STEPS; BUT ONCE YOU'RE THIS BIG AND I CAN KEEP YOU IN MY POCKET AT ALL TIMES, YOUR FRIEND VALERIAN WILL BE VERY COOPERATIVE! HA! HA!

IF I TRY TO DO SOMETHING NOW, I'LL BE FRIED BEFORE I CAN EVEN BLINK.

IN A STRANGELY MURKY LIGHT...

... LAURELINE BEGINS...

... TO SHRINK...

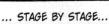

... STAGE BY STAGE...

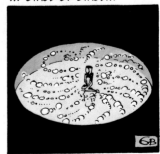

INSIDE THE CABIN, EVERYONE'S ATTENTION IS FIXED UPON THIS STRANGE SIGHT AS THE FINAL STAGE APPROACHES. FASCINATED, XOMBUL HAS RELAXED HIS VIGILANCE...

... SUDDENLY, SCHROEDER CRIES OUT...

NOW, VALERIAN!

CLING

STRUCK BY THE DEAFENING SOUND WAVES THAT FLOOD THE CABIN, XOMBUL AND THE ROBOTS BEGIN THRASHING ABOUT WILDLY.

AND AMIDST THE GENERAL CONFUSION, AFTER HAVING SHUT OFF THE M.M...

M.M
STOP
1 2 3 4 5

... VALERIAN RUSHES TO LAURELINE'S AID.

LAURELINE!

MEANWHILE, INSIDE THE CABIN, THE INFERNAL DIN IS STILL RINGING.

THAT'S ENOUGH, NOW! BRING THAT THING DOWN BEFORE WE GO DEAF!

LAURELINE!!!

HOW ARE YOU FEELING, LAURELINE?... TALK TO ME; SAY SOMETHING.

8A

BUT I AM TALKING TO YOU, YOU IDIOT! I CAN'T SHOUT ANY LOUDER!!! DO SOMETHING! HELP ME! I'VE HAD ENOUGH... THIS KIND OF THINGS ALWAYS HAPPENS TO THE GIRLS!

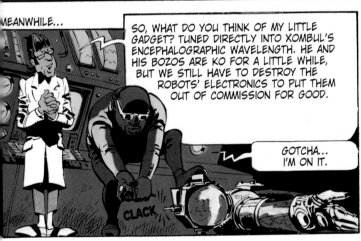

MEANWHILE...

SO, WHAT DO YOU THINK OF MY LITTLE GADGET? TUNED DIRECTLY INTO XOMBUL'S ENCEPHALOGRAPHIC WAVELENGTH. HE AND HIS BOZOS ARE KO FOR A LITTLE WHILE, BUT WE STILL HAVE TO DESTROY THE ROBOTS' ELECTRONICS TO PUT THEM OUT OF COMMISSION FOR GOOD.

GOTCHA... I'M ON IT.

CLACK

FINALLY...

THERE, IT'S DONE. THEY'RE ALL BRAIN DEAD NOW!

WHAT ABOUT ME? WHAT BECOMES OF ME NOW, HUH?!

HMM... IT'S AN ANNOYANCE, OF COURSE. THE M.M. ONLY WORKS ONE WAY...

... BUT SINCE THE PROCEDURE WASN'T COMPLETED, YOU WILL GROW BACK TO YOUR NORMAL SIZE LITTLE BY LITTLE. IT SHOULD ACTUALLY BE QUICK...

YOU SEE, EVERYTHING WILL BE FINE!

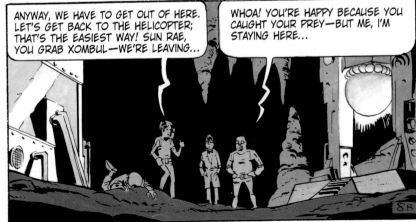

ANYWAY, WE HAVE TO GET OUT OF HERE. LET'S GET BACK TO THE HELICOPTER; THAT'S THE EASIEST WAY! SUN RAE, YOU GRAB XOMBUL—WE'RE LEAVING...

WHOA! YOU'RE HAPPY BECAUSE YOU CAUGHT YOUR PREY—BUT ME, I'M STAYING HERE...

8B

OK, YOU STAY. I HAVEN'T FORGOTTEN OUR AGREEMENT: YOU KEEP THE GADGETS AND I HAVE XOMBUL!

SEE YOU, AND GOOD LUCK!

ER... I'M COMING WITH Y...

NO YOU'RE NOT! YOU'RE STAYING HERE WITH ME. I NEED SOME TUTORING IN PHYSICS AND CHEMISTRY...

A BIT LATER...

I DON'T LIKE LEAVING SCHROEDER. BUT WE MUST GET TO BRASILIA! I DON'T KNOW WHAT THE RANGE OF THAT CHOPPER IS, BUT WE'RE BOUND TO FIND A WAY TO KEEP GOING...

SURE...

... AND THEN, MAYBE ONCE WE'RE BACK IN GALAXITY, YOU COULD FIND A FEW MINUTES IN YOUR BUSY SCHEDULE TO TRY AND GIVE ME BACK MY NORMAL SIZE, RIGHT?

BUT... IT'S NOT MY FAULT IF... HEY, WHAT'S THAT NOISE BEHIND US?

HEY

YOU COULD HAVE WAITED FOR ME! IT'S A GOOD THING I MANAGED TO LOSE YOUR FRIEND INSIDE THE MAINFRAME...

THEN LET'S KEEP GOING. I CAN FEEL XOMBUL STARTING TO MOVE...

BUT, AT THE EXIT...

CURSES! THEY WERE TOO FAR; MY INVENTION DIDN'T HAVE ANY EFFECT ON THEM THROUGH THAT MUCH ROCK...

BY VENUS! I'D FORGOTTEN ABOUT THESE GUYS!

LET ME GO, YOU BRUTISH OAF!

STOP SQUIRMING LIKE THAT DOWN THERE; I'M GOING TO LOSE MY GRIP! VALERIAN, MAKE HIM STOP!

OH, ENOUGH, YOU TWO! IF YOU THINK IT'S EASY TO CARRY YOU AROUND!

WE CAN GET TO THE MESA THIS WAY...

XOMBUL, STAY PUT OR I'LL KNOCK YOU OUT!

STOP BOM

THERE, HE'S QUIET NOW! HANG ON, LAURELINE, WE'RE RUNNING!

VALERIAN!!!

VALERIAN! YOU'VE BEEN HIT!

IT'S NOTHING, A SURFACE BURN! TOO BAD ABOUT XOMBUL! WE HAVE TO ESCAPE QUICKLY! THEY WANT US DEAD, NOW!

WHAT ARE YOU WAITING FOR?! GO AFTER THEM!

AND ATOP THE BARREN MESA, A LONG RACE BEGINS...

NOW, WHAT ON EARTH IS THIS CONTRAPTION?

A SMALL ANTI-GRAVITY VEHICLE. FORTUNATELY FOR US, I HAVEN'T FINISHED WORKING ON IT. IT MOVES AT A SNAIL'S PACE...

THE FLIGHT CONTINUES. STUMBLING AT EVERY STEP, VALERIAN HEADS DOWN INTO A MAZE OF CANYONS...

WE CAN'T GO ON LIKE THIS; IT'D BE MADNESS! THESE MACHINES ARE TIRELESS, WHEREAS WE...

LET'S HIDE OVER THERE...

SOON...

WE HAVE A CHANCE. THEIR RADAR IS AN OLD ONE I SCROUNGED UP, AND IT ISN'T MUCH GOOD... LET'S HOPE THEY'LL GO ON INTO THE MAIN CANYON...

SHHH... WHAT'S WITH YOU? MUST YOU MOVE AROUND LIKE THAT?

NUTS! I'M NOT MOVING— I'M GROWING !!!

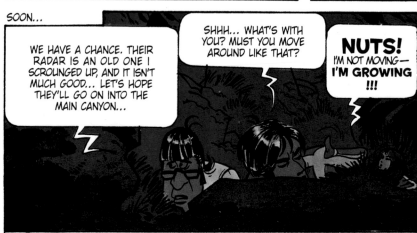

AFTER A FEW ANXIOUS MINUTES...

THAT'S IT ... THEY'RE GONE!

I LOOK LIKE A SCARECROW NOW!

STRANGE!... YOUR CLOTHES MUST HAVE GROWN SLOWER THAN YOUR BODY. COME ON; WE'LL TAKE THE OTHER CANYON...

THE GROUP RESUMES ITS TREK...

WHAT DO WE DO NOW, VALERIAN?

I SIMPLY MUST GET XOMBUL BACK. WE'LL HAVE TO RETURN TO ATTACK THE BASE IN FORCE. BUT HE MUST HAVE DUG IN TO WAIT FOR US!

ALL NIGHT LONG, IN UNNATURAL HEAT, THEY WALK ON...

HOW DO YOU FEEL, LAURELINE?

WELL, I'M BEAT...

OH, I'M A BIG GIRL NOW... YOU'RE THE ONE WHO NEEDS ATTENTION, WITH YOUR WOUND...

FINALLY, AT DAWN, AFTER ONE LAST EXHAUSTING CLIMB...

DOWN THERE! A RANCH!

BUT AS THE THREE FUGITIVES STRUGGLE TO REACH THE HOUSE, A STRANGELY PEACEFUL SOUND GREETS THEM...

TING TING TING

HEY! YOU'VE GOT VISITORS!

TING

IS THERE ANYONE ELSE HERE?

NOPE. THEY'RE ALL GONE. I'M THE LAST ONE LEFT. BUT RINGING MEALTIME IS AN OLD HABIT. AND IT BRINGS A LITTLE LIFE...

ANYWAY, WELCOME TO MY HOME. COME ON IN AND LET'S EAT.

LATER...

DID YOU COME A LONG WAY?

FROM YELLOWSTONE. BUT WE HAD SOME TROUBLE ON THE WAY...

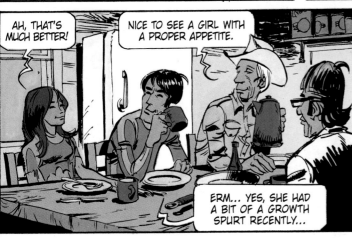

AH, THAT'S MUCH BETTER!

NICE TO SEE A GIRL WITH A PROPER APPETITE.

ERM... YES, SHE HAD A BIT OF A GROWTH SPURT RECENTLY...

WHAT ABOUT YOU? HOW COME YOU'RE STILL HERE?

OH, I'VE LIVED HERE ALL MY LIFE! THIS IS MY RANCH. BUT I CAN SEE THIS IS THE END. JUST YESTERDAY I LOST TWO HUNDRED HEAD OF CATTLE TO A FOREST FIRE. THE EARTH SHAKES EVERY DAY, AND THE QUAKES KEEP GETTING STRONGER...

EVERYTHING'S DRIED OUT WITH THIS HEAT. WHAT CATTLE I HAVE LEFT ARE STARVING TO DEATH...

WHY DON'T YOU LEAVE WITH US? YOU CAN BE OUR GUIDE UNTIL WE FIND A TOWN...

ALL RIGHT, BOY... I GUESS THERE'S NOTHING KEEPING ME HERE ANYMORE. ONCE THE LITTLE LADY'S DONE PATCHING YOU UP, SHE CAN LOOK INTO THAT TRUNK OVER THERE. THERE ARE SOME OLD CLOTHES INSIDE THAT SHOULD FIT HER. IN THE MEANTIME, I'LL SADDLE THE HORSES. I HAVE A TRUCK, BUT IT'S OUT OF GAS... SO... YOU CAN RIDE, CAN'T YOU?

95

BRAVING THE ALREADY SCORCHING HEAT, THE OLD MAN HEADS TO THE CORRAL. ALMOST CONSTANT TREMORS RUN THROUGH THE EARTH'S CRUST...

WHOA! EAAASY!!

CRRR...

...AND INSIDE THE HOUSE...

LOOK OUT!

THE GROUND SHOOK AGAIN...

YEAH. CAN'T HELP BUT WONDER HOW THIS IS GOING TO END...

BADLY. VERY BADLY, I CAN ASSURE YOU...

EVERYTHING ON EARTH HAS BEEN THROWN OUT OF BALANCE BY THE GREAT EXPLOSION. VOLCANOES ARE BECOMING ACTIVE EVERYWHERE, AND I EXPECT TITANIC EARTHQUAKES TO STRIKE...

YESTERDAY, THE BASE'S SEISMOGRAPHS WENT HAYWIRE.

SADDLE UP! WE'RE GONNA TRY TO MAKE IT TO HIGHWAY 89.

13A

SOON, ACROSS THE DEVASTATED LANDSCAPE, WENDING THEIR WAY PAST CRACKS AND CHASMS OLD AND NEW, THE FOUR RIDE FORWARD THROUGH TERRIBLE DANGER...

13B

AT LAST, THE HIGHWAY IS IN SIGHT...

...BUT THE SIGHT IT OFFERS IS NOT A COMFORTING ONE.

WHAT'S GOING ON?

NO ONE KNOWS. WE'VE BEEN STUCK HERE FOR HOURS. PROBABLY AN ACCIDENT FURTHER NORTH.

THE CHILDREN ARE HUNGRY. DO YOU KNOW IF WE'RE NEAR A TOWN?...

AND EVERYONE'S GOING TO RUN OUT OF GAS TOO...

IT'S TERRIBLE!!!

YES! AND IT'S PROBABLY THE SAME ON EVERY HIGHWAY NOT YET UNDER WATER. LET'S GO CHECK WHAT'S GOING ON FURTHER DOWN THE ROAD.

THREE MILES FURTHER ON...

THE CAR BEFORE US FELL IN IT!!! IT JUST OPENED, LIKE THAT...

NO WAY TO GET AROUND IT! BUT IT'S NOT TOO WIDE. WE NEED TO MAKE A LOG BRIDGE.

I CAN HELP WITH THAT! ROUND UP A FEW VOLUNTEERS TO HELP WHILE I GO GET MY AXE.

SOON...

AND...

NICE AND SLOW... YEAH, THAT'S IT!...

OK! NOW LET'S GET THE HORSES ACROSS IN A TRUCK AND GO ON TOWARDS JACKSON ... IF THAT'S STILL POSSIBLE.

AND AFTER A HARD RIDE...

I WONDER WHAT THE MILITARY AND POLICE ARE DOING. ALL THESE POOR PEOPLE NEED TO BE GUIDED AND FED...

GOOD HEAVENS!

WELL, AS REGARDS THE POLICE, THERE'S MY ANSWER. THUGS AND LOOTERS HAVE BEEN AT WORK HERE TOO.

I KNOW WHERE THE MILITARY BASE IS. LET'S GO...

THIS IS IT!

MUSIC?!! I DIDN'T EXPECT THAT!! LET'S GO HAVE A LOOK!

ARE YOU IN COMMAND HERE?

YESSIR!

I COMMAND EVERYONE HERE, 'CEPT THERE ISN'T A SOUL LEFT!... THEY ALL DESERTED AT THE FIRST BIG TREMOR—THOSE VALIANT SOLDIERS OF THE US ARMY! SO WHAT DO Y'ALL WANT ME TO DO ON MY OWN, HUH?...

GOOD THING I HAD MY PERSONAL STASH OF BOURBON, TOBACCO, AND BATTERIES FOR MY TUNES... THE GOOD LIFE, YOU KNOW...

DO YOU HAVE ANY IDEA WHAT THE SITUATION IS IN TOWN?!

DON'T CARE! THE EARTH IS KAPUT, ANYWAY. EVERYTHING IS KAPUT. SO GET LOST AND LEAVE ME ALONE!

BACK OUTSIDE...

THAT GUY IS USELESS!

LISTEN, I THINK THIS IS WHERE WE PART WAYS. I KNOW THIS AREA LIKE THE BACK OF MY HAND, AND I'M SURE I COULD BRING A HERD BACK INTO TOWN. AT LEAST IT'LL STAVE OFF FAMINE...

AND I THINK I'LL FIND EVERYTHING I NEED HERE TO GO BACK AND ATTACK XOMBUL'S FORTRESS.

AND GOOD LUCK TO YOU, SON. YOU WATCH YOUR STEP OUT THERE!...

SO LONG, OLD-TIMER. I'M SORRY I CAN'T GO WITH YOU, BUT I HAVE SOMETHING VERY IMPORTANT TO DO. GOOD LUCK!

SCHROEDER, TAKE A JEEP AND TRY TO FILL THE TANK. I'M GOING TO GET SOME WEAPONS. THIS TIME XOMBUL WILL FIND US READY FOR A FIGHT!

INDEED!

I'LL GO SHOPPING TOO, THEN...

JUST WHAT I NEED!

ARMORY NO ENTRANCE

WELL, CAPTAIN? ARE YOU GOING TO BE NICE AND GIVE ME WHAT I ASKED YOU, HMM?...

GIT ON OUTTA HERE, GIRLY, OR I'LL CALL MY MEN!

?

CPT BLACK

...THERE'S NO ONE ELSE HERE— YOU TOLD US YOURSELF. SO...

CLOP PAF

CPT BLACK

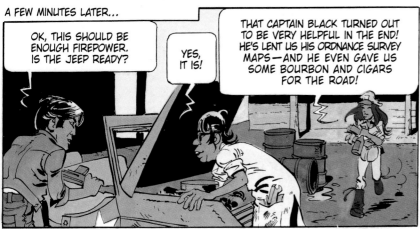

A FEW MINUTES LATER...

OK, THIS SHOULD BE ENOUGH FIREPOWER. IS THE JEEP READY?

YES, IT IS!

THAT CAPTAIN BLACK TURNED OUT TO BE VERY HELPFUL IN THE END! HE'S LENT US HIS ORDNANCE SURVEY MAPS—AND HE EVEN GAVE US SOME BOURBON AND CIGARS FOR THE ROAD!

WE CAN KEEP GOING ALONG THIS ROAD FOR A GOOD WHILE BEFORE TURNING TOWARDS YELLOWSTONE.

LET'S HOPE WE DON'T FIND TOO MANY CRACKS...

A FEW HOURS LATER, AT THE EDGE OF YELLOWSTONE. IN A PROVIDENTIAL JEEP, SALVAGED AND LOADED TO OVERFLOWING WITH VARIOUS WEAPONS AND AMMO...

WE'RE GETTING NEAR... I WONDER IF THERE'S AN ALARM SYSTEM MONITORING THE PARK'S BORDERS.

THERE WAS ONE WHEN THE BASE WAS ACTIVE. XOMBUL MUST STILL BE USING IT.

ENJOY A VISIT TO BEAUTIFUL YELLOWSTONE National Park 10 miles

GOOD! LET'S TAKE ADVANTAGE OF THE DECREASE IN TREMORS TO PROVOKE HIM... I DON'T THINK THE ROBOTS WILL SURVIVE A BAZOOKA.

IT'S RISKY, BUT I DON'T SEE WHAT ELSE TO DO. ANYWAY, WE MUST ACT QUICKLY. THIS PATCH OF SEISMIC CALM IS NOT A GOOD SIGN. SOME DISASTER WORSE THAN ALL THE PREVIOUS ONES IS IN THE MAKING...

THAT'S IT; WE'VE CROSSED INTO THE PARK...

LET'S KEEP OUR EYES PEELED. IF THE ALARM SYSTEM IS STILL WORKING, XOMBUL SHOULDN'T TAKE LONG TO SHOW HIS HAND. IT'S A PITY WE DON'T KNOW WHERE THE DANGER WILL COME FROM...

NOW ENTERING YELLO National

IN THE OPPRESSIVE ATMOSPHERE, THE CAR FORGES ON CAREFULLY, EVERYONE INSIDE ON HIGH ALERT. SUDDENLY...

XOMBUL!!

WELL, WE ASKED FOR IT! LET'S FIND SOME COVER!!!

HURRY!

AND HERE COMES THE INFANTRY... AS EXPECTED!

THE ROBOTS ARE COMING! TAKE CARE OF THE CHOPPER! I'LL HANDLE THE OTHERS!

NO PROBLEM!!!

18A

AND WHILE LAURELINE BEGINS TO FIRE IN BURSTS...

TAKATA TAKATAKATA

PERFECT—THEY HAVEN'T DETECTED ME YET!

... AS LAURELINE, HER AIM OBSTRUCTED BY THE ROCK OVERHANG, CEASES FIRE FOR A MOMENT, A HEAVY, FOREBODING SILENCE DESCENDS...

OH, GREAT! WILL YOU JUST MOVE, YOU DUMB BEAST?!!

I CAN'T HEAR VALERIAN! WHAT'S HE WAITING FOR?

... AND THAT ONE UP THERE? WHY IS HE JUST CIRCLING OVER US NICELY LIKE THAT? IT'S AS IF HE WAS LOOKING FOR A FEW BULLET HOLES...

18B

GOT IT ... BUT THAT WAS CLOSE! AND NOW TO JOIN THE OTHERS...

... MEANWHILE, UNDER THE STILL-CIRCLING AIRCRAFT...

GOT IT!
HEY...

19A

LAURELINE SCORES SEVERAL HITS, BUT THE DROP CONTINUES STEADILY...

WHAT THE DEVIL IS THIS?

THE BUBBLES!!! THE VILLAIN—HE REMEMBERED! LAURELINE, SHOOT!!!

THE BUBBLES?

ANOTHER ONE OF MY INVENTIONS: PRISON-BUBBLES! SHOOT THEM BEFORE THEY FORM; OTHERWISE...

BRATATATATA

OTHERWISE WHAT?

TOO LATE!

19B

... SLOWLY, THE BUBBLES SWALLOW THEIR VICTIMS...

BY SPACE! WE'RE TRAPPED!!!

SAVE YOUR EFFORTS, VALERIAN...

... I MUST SAY, THE PRISON-BUBBLE IS ONE OF MY MOST EXCELLENT IDEAS. A PACIFIC WEAPON, REALLY... AND IMPOSSIBLE TO DEFEAT. A SMALL, SHAPED FORCE FIELD. ALL XOMBUL HAS TO DO NOW IS BRING US BACK REMOTELY TO THE BASE.

WELL... CONGRATULATIONS, SCHROEDER... YOU COULD HAVE TOLD US ABOUT THESE!

YES, WE'RE DONE FOR!

XOMBUL MUST HAVE GOTTEN BACK TO THE LAB. HIS AIRCRAFT WASN'T TOO SERIOUSLY DAMAGED...

GENTLY, THE BUBBLES FLOAT TOWARDS THE BASE...

BUT SUDDENLY, ACROSS A CONVULSING LANDSCAPE, THE VERY EARTH SEEMS TO CATCH ON FIRE...

LOOK! THE ERUPTIONS ARE BEGINNING!

103

THE PRISON-BUBBLES, OUT OF CONTROL, GO OFF THEIR STRAIGHT LINE ITINERARY AND ARE SOON DRIFTING ALONG A RIVER OF LAVA...

HALF-CONSCIOUS, THE PRISONERS ARE TOSSED AROUND BY THE CATACLYSMIC BREATH THAT SWEEPS THE GROUND WITH VOLCANIC ASH...

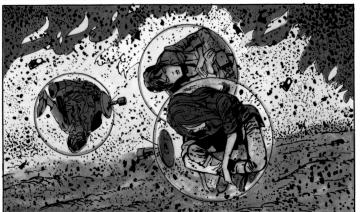 

AND IT'S ONLY MUCH LATER, AFTER THE ERUPTIONS HAVE SLIGHTLY DECREASED IN INTENSITY, THAT THE PRISON-BUBBLES AT LAST COME TO A STOP OVER A SMALL LAKE.

SUDDENLY...

OW!

THE WATER IS SCALDING!

!

PLOOSH SPLASH PLOOSH

DAWN HAS FINALLY COME TO THE TORTURED LANDSCAPE. VALERIAN, LAURELINE AND SCHROEDER HAVE SURVIVED THE HELLISH NIGHT OF FIRE AND ASH...

WHAT HAPPENED?

SOMEONE—OR SOMETHING—SHUT OFF THE FORCE FIELD. WE WERE LUCKY IT DIDN'T HAPPEN ABOVE THE LAVA!

HMM! YOUR BUBBLES ACTUALLY SAVED US FROM DISASTER!

WE HAVE TO GET BACK TO THE BASE... IF IT'S STILL THERE. ANYTHING RATHER THAN STAY OUT IN THIS HELL!

AS IT HAPPENS, WE WENT AROUND IN CIRCLES. THE ENTRANCE TO THE TUNNEL IS UP THERE... A SHORT HALF-HOUR WALK...

SOON...

A LITTLE LATER...

AND MANY HALF-HOURS LATER!!!

MY LAB!!

SUN RAE!

THAT'S RIGHT! IT WAS I WHO FREED YOU AFTER I SAW ON THE SCREEN THAT YOU WERE IN LESS DANGER. IT TOOK ME SOME TIME TO FIGURE OUT HOW THE MACHINE WORKED!.. BUT, HERE YOU ARE AT LAST!

MY LAB! COMPLETELY WRECKED! OH, THE HUMANITY...

ERM... OUR RELATIONS ENDED UP BEING VERY DISAPPOINTING, YOU KNOW. IN ANY CASE, HE BOLTED!

WHAT ABOUT XOMBUL?

WHAT?!

HOURS AGO. I WAS HIDING NEAR THE ROCKET, BECAUSE OF THOSE DAMNED ROBOTS. I SAW XOMBUL RUSH TO IT AT THE FIRST TREMOR, IGNITE THE ENGINE AND.... GOODBYE!

THE ROCKET! WHAT ROCKET??

105

THAT ROCKET THERE!

... THE PERSONAL ROCKET OF THE PRESIDENT OF THE UNITED STATES! HE WAS SUPPOSED TO RETREAT HERE IN CASE OF A NUCLEAR ATTACK, AND THEN LEAVE THE EARTH FOR AN ORBITAL STATION IF ALL WAS LOST.

AND XOMBUL ENDED UP USING IT!

AND WHERE IS THAT ROCKET NOW?

IT WAS ON AUTOPILOT. WHAT YOU'RE SEEING HERE IS A LIVE FEED FROM THE AUTOMATIC CAMERAS ONBOARD THE ORBITAL REFUGE...

YEAH, XOMBUL'S BEEN BUZZING AROUND UP THERE FOR A WHILE!

LOOK! HE TOOK THE DOCUMENTS LOOTED FROM NEW YORK WITH HIM!!

WHAT IS HE WORKING ON?!

THAT I'D LIKE TO KNOW! I WAS AWARE THAT THERE WAS SOME SCIENTIFIC EQUIPMENT UP THERE. BUT IT WAS ALL "TOP SECRET"! EVEN I DIDN'T KNOW WHAT IT WAS ALL ABOUT!

BUT WHAT CAN WE DO?! WE HAVE TO GO GET HIM!!

... OH, YEAH? AND HOW?... HANGING FROM A KITE?...

PFF... GIVE ME A SHOUT WHEN YOU FIGURE OUT SOMETHING...

EVERYONE IS LOST IN DARK THOUGHTS. ON THE SCREENS, OCCASIONALLY BLURRED BY THE TREMORS OF THE EARTH'S CRUST, XOMBUL—THOUSANDS OF MILES AWAY AND UNAWARE THAT HE'S BEING OBSERVED—IS HARD AT WORK.

YOU DON'T LET THINGS GET TO YOU, DO YOU?

BAH! WE'RE STILL BETTER OFF IN HERE THAN OUTSIDE—CAN YOU HEAR ALL THE ERUPTIONS?

SUDDENLY...

WHAT'S THIS THING HERE?!

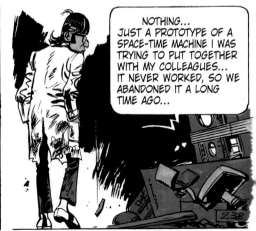

NOTHING... JUST A PROTOTYPE OF A SPACE-TIME MACHINE I WAS TRYING TO PUT TOGETHER WITH MY COLLEAGUES... IT NEVER WORKED, SO WE ABANDONED IT A LONG TIME AGO...

ARE YOU THINKING WHAT I'M THINKING, THEN?

YES! BUT IT'S IMPOSSIBLE! THE FIRST MACHINE WAS INVENTED IN 2314, AND WE'RE IN 1986! SCHROEDER MIGHT BE A GENIUS, BUT STILL...

THIS THING ISN'T THAT GREAT!... THE ENGINEERING WILL NEED A LOT OF HELP.

IT'S WORTH A TRY—IF WE MODIFY ALL THE CIRCUITRY!

HUH, WHAT...?

WHAT ARE YOU TRYING TO DO?? YOU DON'T KNOW THE FIRST THING ABOUT THE MECHANICS OF SPACE-TIME...

MAYBE TWO OR THREE SCIENTISTS IN THE WORLD COULD...

AS IT HAPPENS, I DABBLE A BIT!... AND I LOVE TO TINKER... LEAVE US TO IT, NOW. YOU HEAD DOWN TOO, SUN RAE!

OK, OK...

AND SHORTLY AFTERWARDS...

OK, I SEE WHAT'S WRONG. IT WAS ACTUALLY THE SUBJECT OF MY ENTRANCE EXAM TO THE SPATIO-TEMPORAL SERVICE... EASY FOR US, BUT IMPOSSIBLE FOR PEOPLE OF THE 20TH CENTURY TO SOLVE! LET'S GET TO IT—WRITE DOWN: ...

GO AHEAD!

... A STRANGE PARALLEL RACE BEGINS...

HOW'S XOMBUL DOING?

IT LOOKS LIKE HE'S USING THE DOCUMENTS TO DO SOME FINE-TUNING!

244

I'LL CHECK THE STATION'S COORDINATES. IN THE MEANTIME, FIND US SOME SPACESUITS AND BRING THE OTHERS...

OK! THERE'S BOUND TO BE SOMETHING LIKE THAT IN A BASE LIKE THIS!

SOON...

I'VE GOT EVERYTHING... YOU?

ALL DONE! IT'S UP TO YOU NOW, LAURELINE!

YOU'RE MAD! IT CAN'T WORK, IT'S A MATHEMATICAL IMPOSSIBILITY!

BAH! IF WE STAY HERE, WE'RE DONE FOR ANYWAY!

WE RISK INSTANT DISINTEGRATION! I'M WARNING Y...OUCH!

POK POK POK

FINALLY, AFTER SOME HASTY LAST-MINUTE PREPARATIONS...

POOR SCHROEDER, POOR SUN RAE... UNPLEASANT METHODS, BUT WE COULDN'T SIMPLY LEAVE THEM HERE...

... NO MORE THAN WE COULD LET THEM SEE WHERE WE'RE GOING! COME ON, HURRY! TIME TO GO—EVERYTHING IS COLLAPSING HERE...

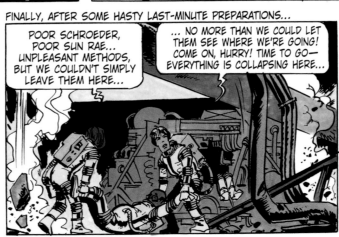

OK! EVERYTHING'S SET. IGNITION!

245

FOR THE FIRST TIME IN EARTH'S HISTORY, HUMAN BEINGS DIVE INTO THE VORTEX OF SPACE-TIME...

... INSTANTANEOUSLY, VALERIAN AND LAURELINE FIND THEMSELVES FLOATING IN SPACE, NEAR THE SECRET STATION WHERE XOMBUL HAS TAKEN REFUGE, THOUSANDS OF MILES FROM EARTH...

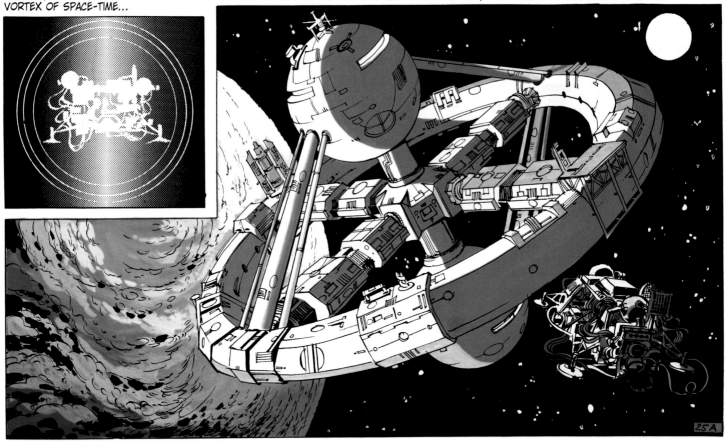

IT WORKED!!! I CAN TELL YOU NOW: I DIDN'T REALLY TRUST THIS JURY-RIGGED THING OF YOURS...

ME, NEITHER— BUT WE'RE NOT DONE YET! LOOK AFTER OUR FRIENDS; I'M GOING AFTER XOMBUL.

I'VE BEEN AFTER HIM FOR SO LONG...

OPTING FOR THE DIRECT APPROACH, VALERIAN ENTERS THE STATION THROUGH THE HATCH...

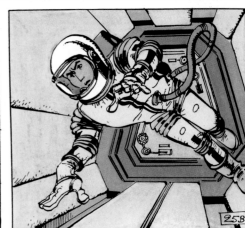

AND...

IT'S OVER, XOMBUL!!! I'M TAKING YOU BACK TO GALAXITY!

VALERIAN!!!

I HAD A HUNCH ABOUT WHAT YOU'D COME TO THE 20TH CENTURY TO FIND: THE FIRST TIME MACHINE. TOUGH LUCK: I'M THE ONE WHO FOUND IT! JUST LOOK AT HOW I GOT HERE... YOU SHOULD HAVE PAID MORE ATTENTION TO SCHROEDER'S DISCARD PILE... EVEN HIS FAILURES ARE IMPRESSIVE!

THAT'S TRUE... BUT HERE, I HAD EVERYTHING AT HAND: THE PLANS RECOVERED FROM THE UN WERE THOSE OF A SPACE-TIME MACHINE THAT THE GREATEST SCIENTISTS HAD WORKED ON. I JUST FINISHED BUILDING IT...

... AND I WAS ABOUT TO RETURN TO EARTH. WITH MY MACHINE AND MY WEAPONS, I COULD HAVE SAVED HUMANITY... TRAVELLED THROUGH HISTORY AT WILL... CHANGED WHAT I DEEMED BAD... BROUGHT ORDER! I, ALONE, COULD HAVE GUIDED THIS INSANE WORLD TOWARDS A GLORIOUS FUTURE! AND TO THINK MY MACHINE WILL NEVER BE USED...

264

SUDDENLY...

HA! HA!... YOU HAVEN'T HEARD THE LAST FROM ME!

DON'T DO THIS—ARE YOU CRAZY?!! A MACHINE FROM THE 20TH CENTURY **CANNOT** WORK!...

... DISREGARDING VALERIAN'S WARNING, XOMBUL ATTEMPTS TO LAUNCH HIMSELF THROUGH SPACE-TIME...

THE FOOL!!!

... FOR A SPLIT SECOND, HIS MACHINE—UNABLE TO MAKE THE JUMP—MATERIALISES OVER THE STATION'S RING.

BUT...

268

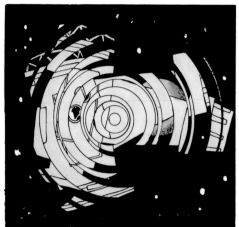

... IN THE ETERNAL SILENCE OF SPACE, BEFORE VALERIAN'S HORRIFIED EYES, VEHICLE AND PASSENGER ARE MERCILESSLY DESTROYED BEFORE DRIFTING AWAY AS SCATTERED DEBRIS...

YOU LOST, XOMBUL! AND IT WAS YOUR OWN FAULT: YOU DIDN'T KNOW ANYTHING ABOUT SPACE-TIME MACHINES!!! ALL RIGHT, NOW'S NOT THE TIME TO GET EMOTIONAL. MISSION ACCOMPLISHED. WE SHOULD GET BACK TO EARTH...

STILL... A QUICK LOOK AT ALL THIS!

AFTER A QUICK INSPECTION...

THESE IMAGES! THESE ARE THE DOCUMENTS I WAS SHOWN IN GALAXITY BEFORE I LEFT... NOW I UNDERSTAND!

IN SEVERAL CENTURIES, WHAT STARTED ME ON THIS MISSION WILL BE DISCOVERED HERE. THEN EVERYTHING IS SORTED. THE CIRCLE IS COMPLETE...

A LITTLE LATER...

DID YOU SEE WHAT HAPPENED TO XOMBUL?

YES... IT WASN'T YOUR FAULT. COME ON—THE MACHINE IS READY TO REMATERIALISE IN BRASILIA...

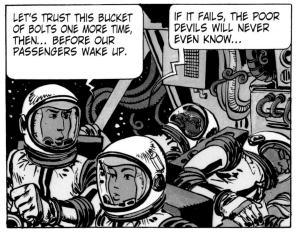

LET'S TRUST THIS BUCKET OF BOLTS ONE MORE TIME, THEN... BEFORE OUR PASSENGERS WAKE UP.

IF IT FAILS, THE POOR DEVILS WILL NEVER EVEN KNOW...

SOON AFTER, NEAR BRASILIA...

OW! MY HEAD... WHERE ARE WE?

WHAT HAPPENED? WHERE'S XOMBUL...?

IT'S ALL OVER! COME THIS WAY; I'LL EXPLAIN... LAURELINE, YOU KNOW WHAT TO DO...

LISTEN, SCHROEDER, YOU'RE PROBABLY ONE OF THE FEW MINDS IN THE 20TH CENTURY ABLE TO ACCEPT WHAT I'M ABOUT TO SAY... AND TO KEEP IT TO YOURSELF. THIS MACHINE YOU JUST CLIMBED OUT OF? IT JUST MADE A JUMP THROUGH SPACE-TIME—AND I MYSELF AM A TRAVELLER FROM THE FUTURE...

COME ON! THAT'S IMPOSSIBLE! ALL THE CALCULATIONS SHOW THAT...

YES... EXCEPT THAT THE CALCULATIONS ARE WRONG... I CAN'T TELL YOU MORE THAN THAT—IT'S UP TO THE PEOPLE OF TODAY'S EARTH TO SOLVE THE PROBLEM. GO TO BRASILIA, SCHROEDER... THERE, YOU WILL JOIN THE GREATEST SCIENTISTS OF THIS TIME... AND YOU HAVE YOUR WORK CUT OUT FOR YOU!

AT LEAST LET ME HAVE A LOOK AT THE MACHINE!

LOOK AT THE MACHINE? GO AHEAD. UNFORTUNATELY, I PUT IT BACK THE WAY YOU'D LEFT IT...

YOU VANDALS! YOU RETROGRADES!!! IT MIGHT TAKE HUNDREDS OF YEARS TO FIND...

MAYBE!... BUT, BEING FROM THE FUTURE DOESN'T GIVE US THE RIGHT TO CHANGE THE PAST!

AT LAST...

THEY'RE OFF TO BRASILIA... I WONDER WHAT THEY'LL FIND THERE...

OH, WE CAN TRUST THEM! THEY'RE BOTH THE RESOURCEFUL TYPE—AND EARTH NEEDS PEOPLE LIKE THAT!

LATER, AT THE UNIVERSITY OF BRASILIA...

... THANK YOU FOR YOUR WELCOME, GENTLEMEN! I DO BELIEVE I HAVE A FEW RESEARCH PROJECTS TO PROPOSE... LET'S GET TO WORK!

... IN THE CITY'S UNDERGROUND...

UNDERSTOOD, BOYS? WE CAN TAKE CONTROL OF THE CITY IN TWO DAYS. HERE'S MY PLAN... LET'S GET TO WORK!

... AND NEARBY:

THERE'S THE ENTRANCE TO THE RELAY... LET'S HEAD BACK TO GALAXITY!

HMM... MAYBE WE COULD MAKE A LITTLE TEMPORAL SIDE TRIP BEFORE RETURNING TO THE 28TH CENTURY... I KNOW THEM. WE WON'T HAVE BEEN BACK FOR AN HOUR BEFORE THEY'LL SEND US BACK TO WORK...

THE END

SCRIPT: P. CHRISTIN
DRAWING: J.C. MEZIERES
69

111

THE EMPIRE OF
A THOUSAND PLANETS

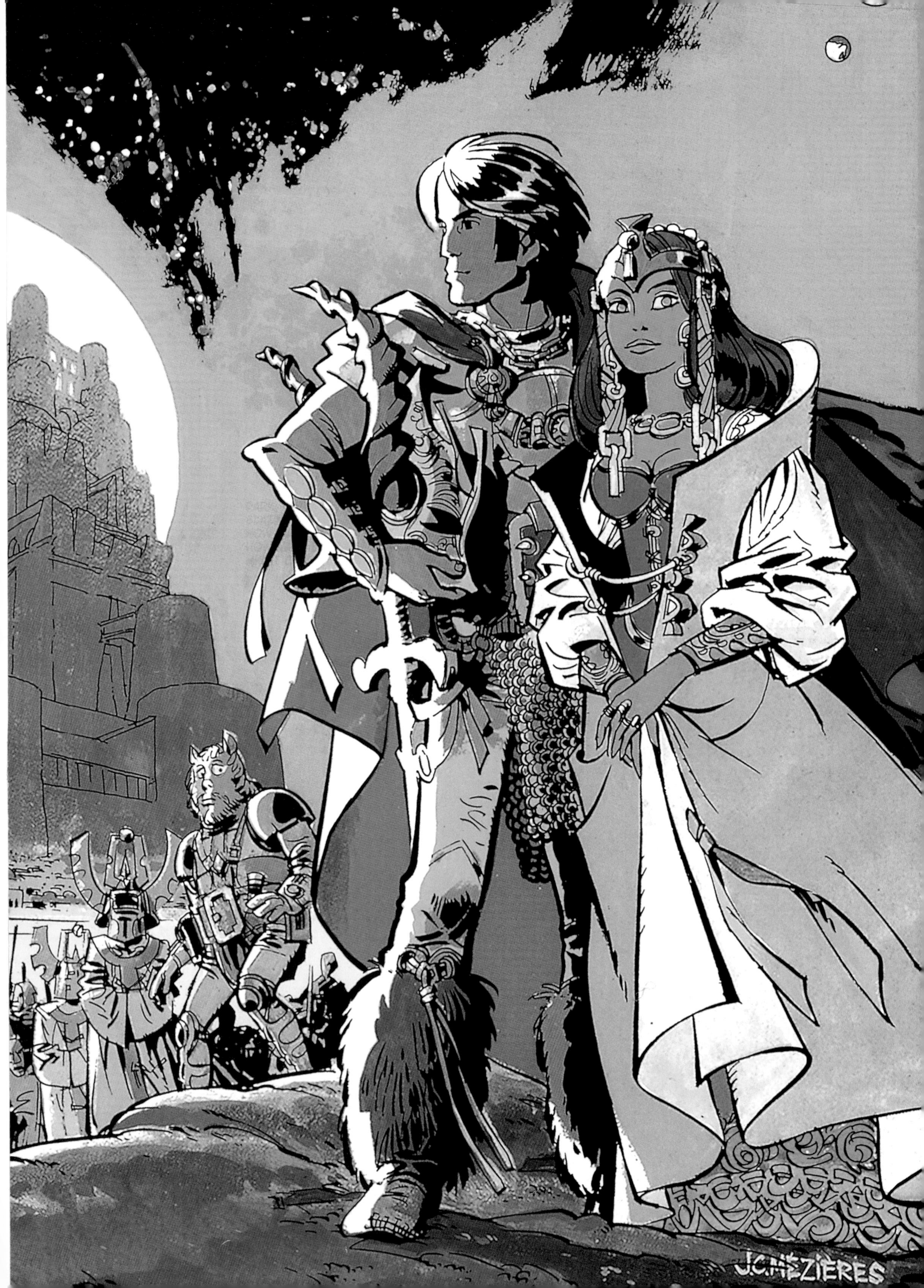
J.C.MÉZIÈRES

IN A DISTANT PART OF
THE GALAXY, ONE PLANET IS
THE HEART OF A HUGE SOLAR
SYSTEM.
　　IT IS
SYRTE THE MAGNIFICENT,
CAPITAL OF THE EMPIRE OF
A THOUSAND PLANETS.

SYRTE AND ITS FABULOUS
IMPERIAL PALACE ARE HOME
TO THE LAST MEMBER OF A
DYNASTY THAT HAS RULED
OVER ALL THE SYSTEM'S
PLANETS SINCE TIME
IMMEMORIAL.

ONLY THE PRINCE'S FAVOURITES
AND AMBASSADORS ACCREDITED
BY IMPERIAL AUTHORITIES EVER
ENTER THE HEAVILY GUARDED
PALACE. THE PEOPLE, OFTEN
GATHERED AT THE DOORSTEP
OF THE BUILDING, HEAR BUT
THE ECHOES OF MYSTERIOUS
CELEBRATIONS...

BUT SYRTE IS, FIRST OF ALL,
THE GREATEST MARKET OF
THE EMPIRE. IN ITS SOUQS,
ARRAYED ALONG THE CANALS,
ONE CAN FIND ANYTHING.
THE MERCHANT GUILD ROAMS
THE SYSTEM TO BRING BACK
COUNTLESS WONDERS...

116

... HYPNOTIC SCHAMIRS FROM PLANET GLIMIUS, INSIDE OF WHICH ONE SLEEPS TO FIND OBLIVION...

... LIVING STONES OF ARPHAL THAT STICK TO ONE'S SKIN TO MAKE THE MOST BEAUTIFUL JEWELS...

... EXCEEDINGLY RARE TELEPATHIC SPIGLICS FROM BLUXTE — PETS THAT LIVE ON THEIR MASTERS' HEADS AND COMMUNICATE TO THEM THEIR CONSTANT BLISS...

... RARE METALS, EXOTIC DELICACIES, MULTICOLOURED FABRICS... IN THE LABYRINTH OF SYRTE'S STREETS, A POPULATION COMING FROM ALL PLANETS BUYS, SELLS, SOMETIMES STEALS...

ONE ALSO COMES TO SYRTE TO CONSULT WITH THE ENLIGHTENEDS, HEALERS OF THE BODY AND SEERS OF THE SOUL, INSCRUTABLE WITHIN THEIR METAL HELMETS...

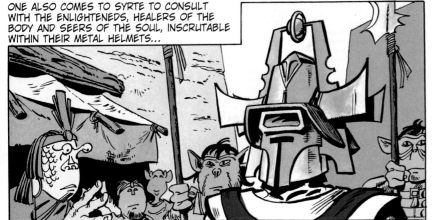

... IT IS SAID THAT THEIR POWER KEEPS GROWING, AND SOME BELIEVE THAT THEY MAY HAVE BECOME THE TRUE MASTERS OF SYRTE. FEW IN NUMBERS, THE ENLIGHTENEDS ARE THE MOST RESPECTED— AND, ABOVE ALL, THE MOST FEARED—GUESTS OF THE PALACE...

... WHEN THEY'RE NOT LIVING INSIDE THEIR TEMPLE-FORTRESSES, DEEP IN THE SYRTIAN JUNGLES.

FINALLY, SYRTE IS ALSO A GIGANTIC SPACEPORT. SINCE THE FIRST DAYS OF INTERPLANETARY TRAVEL, IT HAS WELCOMED SHIPS FROM ALL OVER THE SOLAR SYSTEM. THERE'S NO CUSTOMS, NO SECURITY... ONE COMES TO SYRTE THE MAGNIFICENT UNRESTRAINED, AND ONE LEAVES IT FREELY...

AND HEAVY TRADE VESSELS AS WELL AS LIGHT CRAFTS PEACEFULLY PLY THE SEA ROUTES BETWEEN THE BACK COUNTRY, THE CAPITAL AND THE SPACEPORT. PROPELLED BY THEIR SOLAR SAILS—ON THIS WINDLESS PLANET—THE BOATS THRONG THE CANALS...

AND YET, DESPITE ITS AGE AND GLORY, SYRTE ISN'T WHAT IT ONCE WAS... EVERYWHERE, ABANDONED RUINS, COLLAPSED SEAWALLS AND SILTED-UP HARBOURS...

THE IMPERIAL PALACE ITSELF IS INCREASINGLY RUNDOWN...

IN THE JUNGLE, WHERE POOR FISHERMEN HUNT THE DANGEROUS MARCYAM—A GIGANTIC WATER SNAKE—FOR ITS PRECIOUS SKIN...

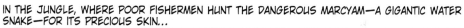

... ONLY THE ENLIGHTENEDS' IMPREGNABLE TEMPLES CONTRAST WITH THE GENERAL POVERTY.

IN SPACE, A FEW LIGHT-YEARS AWAY FROM SYRTE...

118

YOU CAN START RECORDING. IT'S READY.

RIGHT. HI, KIDS! THIS IS VALERIAN, SHIP NUMBER XB982; WE LEFT GALAXITY FOR THE SYRTIAN SYSTEM ON THE 23RD OF SEPTEMBER, 2720...

ORAL REPORT NUMBER FOUR. WE ARE NOW IN THE VICINITY OF SYRTE AND HAVE RECOVERED THE LAST OF THE TERRAN AUTOMATIC PROBES THAT PRECEDED OUR OWN ARRIVAL. AS PLANNED, THE RECORDINGS OF SYRTIAN SPEECH ALLOWED US TO LEARN THE COMMON LANGUAGE BY HYPNO-TEACHING. WE'RE ABOUT TO MAKE THE LAST SPACE/TIME JUMP AND LAND AT SYRTE'S SPACEPORT. NOTHING MUCH TO REPORT FOR THE MOMENT—OVER!

HMM... I DON'T REALLY KNOW, LAURELINE! ANYWAY, WE'RE JUST AGENTS OF THE SPATIO-TEMPORAL SERVICE. OUR JOB IS TO ASSESS WHETHER SYRTE IS A DANGER TO EARTH—OR COULD BECOME ONE...

IT'S A STRANGE FEELING... TO THINK WE'RE ABOUT TO MAKE CONTACT WITH THE FIRST GREAT GALACTIC CIVILISATION OVER WHICH EARTH HAS HAD NO INFLUENCE! DO YOU THINK THERE'S ANY ACTUAL DANGER?

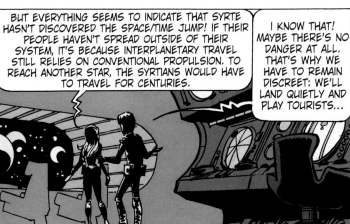

BUT EVERYTHING SEEMS TO INDICATE THAT SYRTE HASN'T DISCOVERED THE SPACE/TIME JUMP! IF THEIR PEOPLE HAVEN'T SPREAD OUTSIDE OF THEIR SYSTEM, IT'S BECAUSE INTERPLANETARY TRAVEL STILL RELIES ON CONVENTIONAL PROPULSION. TO REACH ANOTHER STAR, THE SYRTIANS WOULD HAVE TO TRAVEL FOR CENTURIES.

I KNOW THAT! MAYBE THERE'S NO DANGER AT ALL. THAT'S WHY WE HAVE TO REMAIN DISCREET: WE'LL LAND QUIETLY AND PLAY TOURISTS...

READY FOR THE LAST JUMP?

READY...

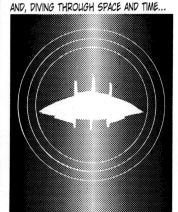

AND, DIVING THROUGH SPACE AND TIME...

... VALERIAN AND LAURELINE'S SHIP MATERIALISES IN A REMOTE CORNER OF THE SYRTIAN SPACEPORT.

SOON...

... VALERIAN AND LAURELINE LEAVE THE SPACEPORT UNIMPEDED AND, ALONGSIDE OTHER TRAVELLERS, HEAD TOWARDS THE CAPITAL.

5A

EVERYTHING'S GOING WELL SO FAR.

YEAH... I'M NOT SURPRISED... MOST SPECIES HERE ARE HUMANOID—WE CAN LOSE OURSELVES IN THE CROWD!

FORTUNATELY, THEY ALSO WEAR ALL KINDS OF OUTFITS! WE'RE BLENDING RIGHT IN...

WHAT A WONDERFUL MARKET! LOOK, IT'S THE JEWELLER'S ALLEY! LET'S GO HAVE A LOOK...

... I HAVE SOME GOLD WITH ME, AND I SAW THAT THEY ACCEPT IT AS CURRENCY HERE.

OH, COME ON! YOU'RE NOT GOING TO START BUYING STUFF, ARE YOU?... FINE...

5B

BRRR... ALL THESE JEWELS YOU STICK ON YOUR SKIN ARE GORGEOUS, BUT I DON'T REALLY FEEL LIKE GOING AROUND WITH CRITTERS ALL OVER ME...

OH, VALERIAN! LOOK!

A WATCH... IT LOOKS VERY OLD. WHAT LOVELY DECORATIONS.

YES... STRANGE... I'VE SEEN VERY SIMILAR ONES AT THE PRE-ATOMIC MUSEUM OF GALAXITY. SO, DO YOU LIKE IT?

5C

YOU'RE SWEET TO BUY IT FOR ME... SMOOCH... IT WORKS, YOU KNOW!

BAH... MISSION EXPENSES! LET'S CHECK OUT THAT GATHERING OVER THERE.

WHAT'S GOING ON?

IS THIS THE FIRST TIME YOU'VE COME TO SYRTE? THEN PAY ATTENTION... THIS IS ONE OF THE MOST FAMOUS OF THE ENLIGHTENEDS. TODAY, HE'S AGREED TO ANSWER QUESTIONS...

... LOOK, A RICH MERCHANT FROM PLANET FLUGIL IS COMING TO CONSULT HIM.

MIGHTY ENLIGHTENED! I CALL UPON YOUR MUNIFICENCE AND BEG AN ANSWER TO THIS QUESTION: WILL I LIVE LONG ENOUGH TO SEE MY BUSINESS PROSPER UNTIL IT IS THE MOST SUCCESSFUL IN THE FIELD THAT IS MINE?

IN THE SILENCE OF THE ATTENTIVE CROWD, A VOICE SOON ECHOES, DEEP IF SLIGHTLY MUFFLED...

HEED MY ANSWER, MERCHANT. YOU WILL DIE IN 100 DAYS... GO BACK TO YOUR WORLD IF YOU WANT TO PUT YOUR AFFAIRS IN ORDER, FOR YOUR ILLNESS...

SUDDENLY, TO EVERYONE'S SURPRISE, THE ENLIGHTENED STOPS, AND...

YOUNG WOMAN! COME NEAR!

WHAT'S GOING ON?

THE ENLIGHTENEDS NEVER SPEAK TO THE COMMON PEOPLE DIRECTLY...

COME NEAR!!!

WHO... ME?!

YES, YOU! WHERE DID YOU FIND THIS OBJECT?...

WELL... HERE! I JUST BOUGHT IT FROM THE MARKET BECAUSE I LIKED IT, AND...

WHAT IS THE PURPOSE OF THIS... ORNAMENT?

TELLING TIME, OF COURSE! THERE'S NOTHING SPECIAL ABOUT THAT!

HEARING THESE WORDS, THE CROWD AROUND LAURELINE BURSTS OUT LAUGHING, WHILE THE ENLIGHTENED TURNS AWAY WITHOUT A FURTHER WORD AND HURRIES OFF TOWARDS THE PALACE...

BUT... WHAT DID I SAY?...

SHUT UP AND LET'S VAMOOSE! WE MUST HAVE BLUNDERED SOMEHOW, BUT I DON'T KNOW HOW.

TELLING TIME! HA! HA! HA!

THAT GIRL'S CRAZY...

DID YOU SEE? THE ENLIGHTENED WAS OFFENDED BY HER IMPERTINENCE. HE'S LEAVING...

121

A SHORT WHILE LATER...

I CAN'T WAIT TO GET BACK TO THE SPACEPORT. NIGHT FALLS QUICKLY ON SYRTE, AND I HAVE THIS FEELING THAT WE'RE BEING FOLLOWED...

FOLLOWED BY WHOM? FOR WHAT REASON? THAT WATCH BUSINESS IS JUST STUPID!

DO YOU SEE THOSE TWO BOATS?... THEY'VE BEEN BEHIND US FOR A GOOD LONG WHILE... WE HAVE TO LOSE THEM!

BOATMAN! TAKE THE CANAL TO THE RIGHT, QUICKLY!

BOM

AND IN THE THICK SYRTIAN NIGHT, A CONFUSED STRUGGLE BEGINS...

QUICKLY OVERWHELMED BY THEIR ASSAILANTS' NUMBERS, VALERIAN AND LAURELINE ARE SOON KNOCKED OUT AND CAPTURED...

IN THE MORNING...

OH, MY HEAD... WHERE ARE WE?

ON A SOLAR-POWERED VESSEL. WE'RE ABOUT TO SET SAIL...

... THROUGH EVER MORE ABUNDANT VEGETATION.

INDEED, THE SHIP SOON BEGINS TO PICK UP SPEED. WITH THE SUNS HIGH OVER THE HORIZON, ITS SAILS FULLY DEPLOYED, IT RACES OVER THE CANALS OF SYRTE...

MUCH LATER, AS A GUARD UNTIES VALERIAN AND LAURELINE...

THESE GUARDS ARE MUTE. NOT MUCH CHANCE OF LEARNING WHAT WE CAN EXPECT FROM THEM...

AND, UNDER CLOSE WATCH...

... CROSSING THE GANGWAY JUST LOWERED TO THE QUAY...

... THE SMALL GROUP ENTERS THE ENLIGHTENEDS' SANCTUARY.

VALERIAN! AN ISOLATED TEMPLE! LIKE THE ONES THE AUTOMATIC PROBES LOCATED AND REPORTED...

HMM... ALL WE KNOW IS THAT THE ENLIGHTENEDS LIVE THERE. WELL, LOOKS LIKE WE'RE ABOUT TO LEARN MORE...

WITH A SIMPLE GESTURE, ONE OF THE GUARDS ACTIVATES
THE MECHANISM THAT OPENS THE MASSIVE FRONT DOOR.

... WHILE THE DOOR CLOSES BEHIND THEM...

... PUSHED FORWARD BY THE GUARDS...

... VALERIAN AND LAURELINE REACH THE TOP OF THE STAIRS.

PFFF... I BET SOMEONE'S ABOUT TO ASK ME FOR THE TIME AGAIN...

YOU AND YOUR WATCH! IT'S PROBABLY BECAUSE OF IT THAT WE'RE HERE...

AFTER WAITING IN SILENCE...

124

... THE QUESTION I'M ABOUT TO ASK YOU, YOUNG WOMAN, IS NOT WHAT YOU'RE EXPECTING. BESIDES, I ALREADY KNOW THE ANSWER TO IT. **ARE YOU FROM EARTH?**

WAY TO GO, LAURELINE! A FINE MESS SHE'S GOT US INTO...

SMART, VALERIAN. TALK ABOUT A COVERT MISSION...

DON'T DENY IT! THIS WATCH, AND THE FACT THAT YOU KNOW ITS PURPOSE, HAVE BETRAYED YOU...

HA HA! YOU'D HAVE TO BE AN EARTHLING TO BUY SUCH AN OBJECT. YOU'D HAVE TO BE UNAWARE THAT ALL INHABITANTS OF THE SYRTIAN SYSTEM HAVE AN INNATE, PERFECT SENSE OF TIME...

WE DON'T KNOW WHY YOU CAME TO SYRTE. BUT WE'LL SOON FIND OUT... WE'RE ALREADY INSPECTING YOUR SPACESHIP...

YOU'LL NEVER BE ABLE TO GET INSIDE OUR SHIP. I SET THE SAFETY LOCK FOR SELF-DESTRUCT!

BE SILENT! HOW VERY MUCH LIKE EARTHLINGS. THEIR PRIDE, THEIR OBSTINACY, THEIR FOLLY! **ACCURSED RACE!** OUR VENGEANCE WILL BE TERRIBLE!!!

VENGEANCE?... BUT WHY? WE COME IN PEACE...

THAT'S ENOUGH! YOU WILL REMAIN HERE AS PRISON-ERS. NO ONE WILL EVER NOTICE YOUR DISAPPEARANCE. WE STILL NEED YOU FOR THE MOMENT; AFTERWARDS...

AFTER THESE OMINOUS WORDS, THE ENLIGHTENED VANISHES INTO THE SHADOWS, WHILE THE THICK BLAST DOOR BEGINS TO DESCEND...

ALL OR NOTHING, LAURELINE!!!

125

AND, SCRAPING THROUGH...

... VALERIAN AND LAURELINE FIND THEMSELVES IN DARKNESS.

ON THE OTHER SIDE, THE GUARDS SEEM TO BE IN THE GRIP OF EXTREME INDECISION, AS IF SCARED AT THE IDEA OF ENTERING THE ENLIGHTENEDS' DEMESNE TO PURSUE THE FUGITIVES...

WHAT DO WE DO NOW?

ANYTHING EXCEPT STAY HERE. NO DOUBT THE GUARDS WILL RAISE THE ALARM SOON! LET'S HEAD TOWARDS THAT LIGHT, THERE...

NO ONE!

AN ENGINE ROOM!!!

BY THE GALAXY!!! THESE TEMPLES ARE ACTUALLY POWER PLANTS!

FURTHER ON...

LABORATORIES NOW! AND RATHER ADVANCED, IT WOULD SEEM...

YES... THEY USE RELIGION AS A FRONT, BUT IT LOOKS LIKE THE ENLIGHTENEDS HAVE COMPLETE CONTROL OVER SYRTE'S SCIENTIFIC EQUIPMENT...

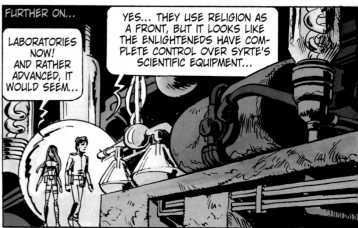

THE STRANGE THING IS THAT EVERYTHING SEEMS ABANDONED! LOOK AT THESE DEVICES... NO ONE'S TOUCHED THEM FOR YEARS... MAYBE EVEN CENTURIES...

THE MACHINERY IS PROBABLY STILL WORKING, THANKS TO SOME SELF-REPAIR SYSTEMS. BUT NOTHING ELSE SEEMS TO BE IN USE... WELL, ANYWAY, WE'LL WORRY ABOUT THAT LATER...

THE IMPORTANT THING FOR THE MOMENT IS TO GET OUT OF HERE. THERE MUST BE SOME AIRCRAFT SOMEWHERE... I DOUBT THE ENLIGHTENEDS ONLY USE SOLAR-POWERED SHIPS...

THEN LET'S GO BACK TO THE POWER PLANT. IF THERE ARE PLANES IN HERE, THAT'S WHERE THEY MUST RECHARGE.

INDEED, A LITTLE LATER...

YOU WERE RIGHT, KIDDO!

HMM... PRETTY STANDARD SETUP, FROM THE NUCLEAR ENGINE TO THE EJECTOR SEAT. I SHOULD BE ABLE TO HANDLE IT...

VALERIAN!

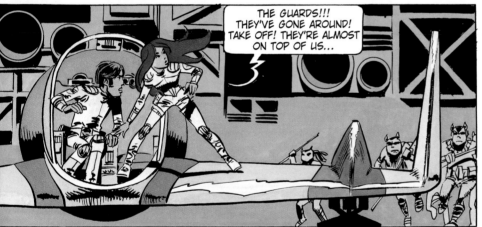

THE GUARDS!!! THEY'VE GONE AROUND! TAKE OFF! THEY'RE ALMOST ON TOP OF US...

HURRY!

TAKE OFF, TAKE OFF!!! EASY FOR YOU TO SAY... I'VE FOUND EVERYTHING EXCEPT THE IGNITION!

THIS ONE?!?

THIS ONE?... NAH...

HEY!!

VALERIAN! THE WALL!!! WATCH IT!!!

127

UNDER THE—FORTUNATELY—ERRATIC FIRE OF THE GUARDS, VALERIAN SOMEHOW MANAGES...

... TO TAKE HIS PLANE THROUGH THE EXIT...

... BEFORE RACING AWAY JUST ABOVE THE FOREST...

OW... A TAD ON THE ROUGH SIDE TODAY, PILOT!...

HAHA!... COME ON, STRAIGHTEN UP! FASTEN YOUR SEATBELT—AND CHECK TO SEE IF WE'RE BEING FOLLOWED...

WELL?

THERE ARE TWO JETS PURSUING US!

SECONDS TICK BY...THE SYRTIAN AIRCRAFT INEXORABLY CLOSE IN ON VALERIAN...

I CAN'T SHAKE THEM... I DON'T KNOW EVERY-THING THIS BIRD CAN DO... HANG ON... THAT STORM FORMATION OVER THERE?! MAYBE I'LL BE ABLE TO LOSE THEM IN THE CLOUDS...

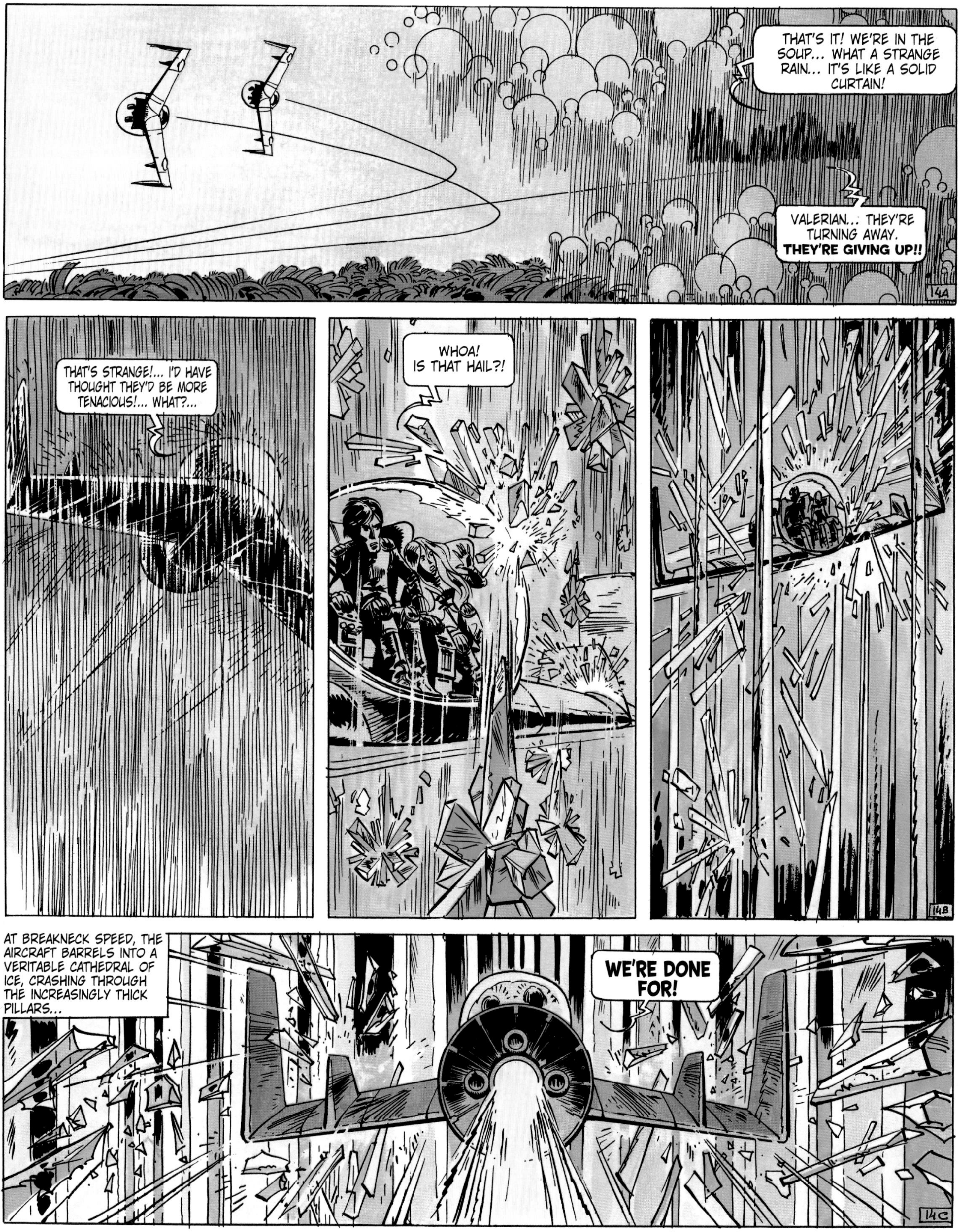
THAT'S IT! WE'RE IN THE SOUP... WHAT A STRANGE RAIN... IT'S LIKE A SOLID CURTAIN!
VALERIAN... THEY'RE TURNING AWAY. **THEY'RE GIVING UP!!**
THAT'S STRANGE!... I'D HAVE THOUGHT THEY'D BE MORE TENACIOUS!... WHAT?...
WHOA! IS THAT HAIL?!
AT BREAKNECK SPEED, THE AIRCRAFT BARRELS INTO A VERITABLE CATHEDRAL OF ICE, CRASHING THROUGH THE INCREASINGLY THICK PILLARS...
WE'RE DONE FOR!

AND, JUST BEFORE THE OUT-OF-CONTROL AIRCRAFT SLAMS INTO A WALL OF ICE...

THE EJECTOR SEAT!!! IT'S OUR LAST CHANCE... WE'RE BAILING OUT!

FINALLY, THE COCKPIT REACHES THE GROUND...

GOOD GRIEF... WE GOT OFF LIGHTLY ON THIS ONE!

YES... NOW I UNDERSTAND WHY OUR PURSUERS TURNED BACK...

THE SYRTIAN WEATHER SYSTEM IS FULL OF SURPRISES. JUST LIKE THE LACK OF WIND, I IMAGINE THESE SUDDEN ICE STORMS ARE THE CONSEQUENCE OF SOME SORT OF ELECTROSTATIC PHENOMENON. SO COLD...

LET'S WALK... OR WE'RE GOING TO FREEZE TO DEATH HERE...

HOLD ME; I'M COLD...

VALERIAN AND LAURELINE BEGIN A SLOW MARCH OVER THE FROZEN TERRAIN, COVERED WITH CRUNCHY FROST HERE, SLIPPERY AS A MIRROR THERE...

BUT SOON, AS SWIFTLY AS THE STORM'S ICY COLD HAD COME, THE CLOUDS DISPERSE AND SYRTE'S TWIN BLAZING SUNS REAPPEAR...

IN AN INSTANT, A STRANGE AERIAL VEGETATION SPRINGS FORTH FROM MILLIONS OF SPORES SUSPENDED IN THE ATMOSPHERE...

DRUNK WITH SMELLS AND COLOURS, VALERIAN AND LAURELINE BARELY NOTICE AS THE THIN CRUST OF ICE BEGINS TO CRACK BELOW THEIR FEET...

HOW WONDERFUL THIS IS, VALERIAN... CAN YOU FEEL THE FLOWERS?! HOW SOFTLY THEY BRUSH AGAINST US...

... THE SYRTIAN CLIMATE IS TRULY FULL OF SURPRISES...

CRACK

WELL! WINTER'S REALLY SHORT ON SYRTE!

YEAH... AT LEAST WE CAN TOUCH BOTTOM HERE...

AS VALERIAN AND LAURELINE STRUGGLE ON THROUGH THE MUDDY WATERS...

HANG IN THERE! SOLID GROUND, STRAIGHT AHEAD!

AAHH!

A MARCYAM!

SUDDENLY, A VOLLEY OF BOLTS COMES OUT OF NOWHERE...

... AND STRIKES THE MAGNIFICENT AND TERRIBLE ANIMAL. AS THE BEAST COLLAPSES IN A SERIES OF MASSIVE CONVULSIONS, VALERIAN AND LAURELINE REACH THE SHORE, EXHAUSTED...

JUST THEN, COMING OUT OF A CLUMP OF TREES...

MARCYAM HUNTERS!!!

I'M EXHAUSTED! TOO MUCH HAS HAPPENED TOO QUICKLY!

A GOOD CATCH TODAY! THE MARCYAMS ALWAYS COME OUT OF THEIR WATERHOLES AFTER STORMS. THE POLLEN FROM THE FLOWERS DRIVES THEM MAD...

ARE YOU GOING TO HUNT MORE?...

WE HAVE ENOUGH DRIED SKINS TO SAIL BACK TO THE CAPITAL. IT'S ALMOST TIME FOR THE FESTIVAL OF THE EMPIRE'S AMBASSADORS! A GOOD TIME TO SELL MANY SKINS...

CAN YOU TAKE US THERE?

WE CAN PAY YOU WITH GOLD...

NO! YOU WILL BE OUR GUESTS. WE LEAVE AT DAWN TOMORROW...

18A

DAY AFTER DAY, IN THE STILL AIR, THE SMALL FLOTILLA FOLLOWS THE CANALS THAT CRISSCROSS THE PLANET. THE LUSH FORESTS GIVE WAY TO CULTIVATED FIELDS...

FINALLY...

AND WE'RE BACK IN SYRTE!

YES... WE LOST A LOT OF TIME GETTING BACK HERE! BUT THAT'S NOT SUCH A BAD THING. THAT WAY, THE ENLIGHTENEDS MUST THINK WE'RE DEAD... HOWEVER, WE'RE GOING TO HAVE TO MAKE SURE WE DON'T REPEAT THE MISTAKES WE MADE WHEN WE FIRST ARRIVED...

18B

133

AT THE FOOT OF THE PALACE'S FORMIDABLE WALLS, VARIOUS BOATS THRONG THE MAIN CANAL, WHICH BUZZES WITH ACTIVITY AS THE TIME OF THE FESTIVAL OF THE AMBASSADORS APPROACHES. AND, AS THE FISHERMEN BUSTLE ABOUT ON THE DOCK AMIDST THE HEADY SCENT OF SPICES, PRECIOUS WOOD ESSENCES AND DRIED SKINS BEING UNLOADED...

WHAT'S YOUR PLAN? MORE COVERT STUFF?

PRECISELY, YOUNG LADY! BEFORE WE DO ANYTHING, WE NEED TO KNOW WHO'S RULING THIS EMPIRE... THE PRINCE OR THE ENLIGHTENEDS? I WANT TO KNOW FOR SURE...

WHAT ABOUT OUR SHIP? YOU ACTUALLY BELIEVE IT'S STILL WAITING FOR US?

OK, THAT'S ENOUGH SARCASM FROM YOU! THERE IS NO WAY WE CAN AFFORD TO SNOOP AROUND A SHIP THAT'S LIKELY UNDER A 'ROUND-THE-CLOCK WATCH! ANYWAY, I'M SURE THE ENLIGHTENEDS HAVEN'T MANAGED TO BREAK IN. THEY WANT IT TOO BADLY TO BLOW IT UP...

THEN... WHAT DO WE DO?

WE'RE GOING TO BUY SOME MORE ELEGANT CLOTHES. AND THEN WE'LL FIND A WAY TO GET INSIDE THE PALACE—BY POSING AS FOREIGN NOBLES INVITED TO THE PARTY.

A LITTLE LATER...

I MUST SAY, I REALLY LIKE SYRTE! SUCH BEAUTIFUL FABRICS! HOW DO I LOOK?

VERY NICE! COME TAKE A LOOK...

WHAT'S THE RUSH...?

LOOK AT THAT PROCESSION OVER THERE... THIS IS THE PERFECT OPPORTUNITY TO INFILTRATE THE PALACE...

... WE'LL MERGE WITH THAT GROUP OF VISITORS...

TRY TO LOOK REGAL, OK?... WE HAVE TO IMPRESS THE GUARDS!

YEAH, RIGHT!!!

BUT...

RATS. SO MUCH FOR THAT PLAN...

THE GUARDS MUST HAVE SOME TRICK TO IDENTIFY AUTHORISED VISITORS... THAT MACHINE...

CORRECT! IT'S AN AUTOMATIC DECODER, AND EVERY AMBASSADOR MUST PRESENT HIS PERSONAL SEAL TO IT...

I DID TRY TO FORGE SOME FOR MY OWN USE... BUT IT DIDN'T WORK...

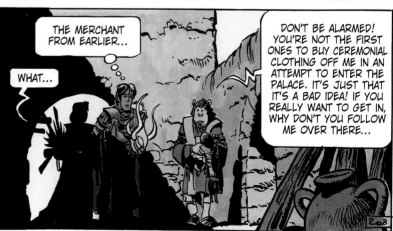

THE MERCHANT FROM EARLIER...

WHAT...

DON'T BE ALARMED! YOU'RE NOT THE FIRST ONES TO BUY CEREMONIAL CLOTHING OFF ME IN AN ATTEMPT TO ENTER THE PALACE. IT'S JUST THAT IT'S A BAD IDEA! IF YOU REALLY WANT TO GET IN, WHY DON'T YOU FOLLOW ME OVER THERE...

ACCESS TO THE PALACE WASN'T ALWAYS SO DIFFICULT. BUT NOW, THE RULES ARE SO STRICT THAT EVEN FOOD AND LUXURY ITEMS ARE HOISTED UP THE WALLS LIKE THAT... THEY'RE AFRAID OF PRYING EYES UP THERE...

WHO ARE YOU TO SPEAK IN SUCH A WAY?

I'M ELMIR, HUMBLE MERCHANT OF SYRTE—AT YOUR SERVICE!... AND I HAVE AN OFFER FOR YOU. AFTER NIGHTFALL, I CAN HELP YOU ENTER THE PALACE WITH A SHIPMENT OF SCHAMIRS. IN EXCHANGE...

... I WANT SOME INFORMATION ON THE ENLIGHTENEDS! FOR VARIOUS REASONS, I'D RATHER CALL UPON STRANGERS SUCH AS YOURSELVES. IF YOU MANAGE TO EXIT THE PALACE AGAIN—AND THAT PART IS YOUR PROBLEM—YOU CAN FIND ME IN BLACK STREET. IF YOU BRING ME ANY INFORMATION, I'LL BE ABLE TO HELP YOU AGAIN...

WELL, I'LL BE... COULD IT BE A TRAP...? IT'D BE A CRUDE ONE...

WHERE ARE THE ENLIGHTENEDS?

IN THE OTHER WING OF THE MAIN BUILDING, ACROSS FROM THE PRINCE'S HUGE CHAMBERS, IT IS SAID. I'D LIKE TO KNOW EXACTLY WHAT'S GOING ON THERE... WHAT MACHINES THEY POSSESS... IN SHORT, ANYTHING AND EVERY-THING OF INTEREST. SO...?

ALL RIGHT! YOU HAVE A DEAL...

A LITTLE LATER, IN THE GROWING DARKNESS...

BE CAREFUL NOT TO LET THE SCHAMIRS FULLY CLOSE OVER YOU! THEIR HYPNOTIC FUMES WOULD MAKE YOU FORGET WHO YOU ARE... GOOD LUCK. AND REMEMBER: ELMIR, MERCHANT, BLACK STREET...

AND...

THERE... WE JUST HAVE TO WAIT NOW...

FINALLY, AFTER A LONG WAIT, THE SHIPMENT OF SCHAMIRS IS HOISTED IN A GREAT CREAKING OF PULLEYS...

AFTER A ROUGH LANDING...

... THE TRIP ENDS IN AN ENORMOUS STOCKROOM. STRUGGLING TO BREATHE, AND FIGHTING THE CLOYING INTOXICATION THAT SPREADS THROUGH HIM, VALERIAN WAITS. AS HE GAZES AT THE DISTANT LIGHT OF A TORCH, HE LOSES ALL NOTION OF TIME...

... UNTIL, REASSURED BY THE SILENCE...

LAURELINE... WHERE ARE YOU?

BY SPACE!!! THIS BROKEN SHELL UNDER THE OTHERS MUST HAVE BEEN HERS. WHAT HAPPENED TO HER?... HYPNOTISED, MAYBE...

WHERE DO THESE STAIRS LEAD?... MUSIC... SOUNDS LIKE A PARTY... MAYBE SHE WENT THIS WAY, UNAWARE... I'M GOING...

IT'S A GRANDIOSE SIGHT THAT GREETS VALERIAN AT THE TOP OF THE STAIRS. AMONG THE RUSTLE OF CONVERSATIONS, HE WALKS UNIMPEDED THROUGH GROUPS OF GUESTS, SURROUNDED BY PERFUMES, SOUNDS, AND COLOURS UNKNOWN TO EARTH...

SUCH LUXURY!... LOOK AT THOSE HANGING LODGES...

THIS PALACE MUST BE CHOCK-FULL OF HI-TECH FACILITIES TO MAKE ALL THIS POSSIBLE...

A KHAMAR NECTAR, TRAVELLER?...

ER... YOU COULD SAY THAT...

ER... WITH PLEASURE...

YOU LOOK SURPRISED! COULD IT BE THE FIRST TIME YOU'RE ATTENDING AN IMPERIAL PARTY?...

LOOK UP THERE, UNDER THAT CUPOLA. HIS HIGHNESS PRINCE RAMAL IS ENJOYING HIMSELF! HA! HA!...

BUT... BUT... THAT'S...

LAURELINE!!! I'LL BE...! I'M WILLING TO BELIEVE SHE'S HIGH ON SCHAMIR FUMES, BUT STILL... AND WHAT CAN I DO?!

AH! OUR BELOVED PRINCE'S CUPOLA JUST WENT DARK...

... THE PARTY IS OVER, TRAVELLER...

GOODBYE...

ONLY ONE THING TO DO, NOW THAT I'M HERE. TAKE ADVANTAGE OF THE CONFUSION CAUSED BY THE DEPARTING GUESTS TO PAY THE ENLIGHTENEDS A VISIT...

IN THE DYING LIGHTS OF THE NIGHT'S CELEBRATION, AS THE CUPOLAS GO DARK ONE BY ONE, VALERIAN SNEAKS OUT...

ALL CLEAR, BUT I'D BETTER WATCH FOR PATROLS.

ACCORDING TO THE MERCHANT'S DIRECTIONS, THE ENLIGHTENEDS ARE ON THIS SIDE.

WHAT'S THIS LIGHT? AND THIS MUFFLED SOUND?...

A POWER PLANT JUST LIKE IN THE TEMPLE. BUT THIS ONE IS HUGE... PROBABLY THE PALACE'S NERVE CENTRE...

24A

STILL NO ENLIGHT-TENEDS, EITHER AT THE PARTY OR HERE...

AND FURTHER STILL, AFTER A PATIENT SEARCH...

THAT TOWER OVER THERE... THAT'S PROBABLY IT... WON'T BE EASY TO REACH!

24B

139

WHILE VALERIAN, HIDDEN IN THE SHADOWS, LOOKS UPON THE STRANGE SPECTACLE, THE ENLIGHTENEDS SLOWLY REMOVE THEIR HEAVY HELMETS. WITH SOLEMN GESTURES, ONE OF THEM PREPARES A SLIGHTLY PHOSPHORESCENT BREW, ITS LIGHT ENCROACHING ON THE DARKNESS...

AH, SOME LUCK AT LAST. THEY'RE GATHERED HERE... WHAT ARE THEY DOING?

SUDDENLY, BEFORE DRINKING THE LIQUID THEY HAVE BEEN SERVED, THE ENLIGHTENEDS UTTER IN PERFECT UNISON A PHRASE THAT SEEMS TO BIND THEM IN RITUAL...

SO THAT WE LIVE, AND THAT EARTH DIES!

BUT A SMALL MOVEMENT FROM VALERIAN CAUSES A PORTCULLIS TO SLAM ONTO THE NARROW LEDGE...

CLANG

THERE! SOMEONE!

RATS! AN ELEC-TRONIC SENSOR!

HURRIEDLY PUTTING THEIR HELMETS BACK ON, THE ENLIGHTENEDS ATTACK, AND...

AFTER A SHORT STRUGGLE...

140

THE EARTHLING WE BELIEVED LOST!

HE WON'T ESCAPE US THIS TIME. TAKE HIM TO THE INTERROGATION ROOM.

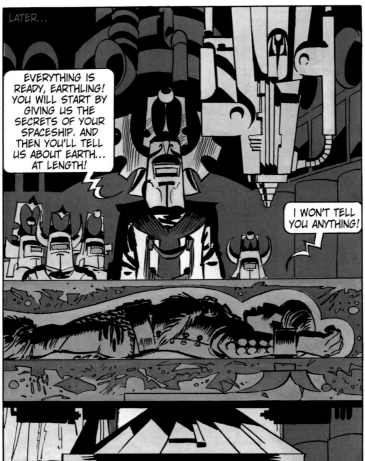

LATER...

EVERYTHING IS READY, EARTHLING! YOU WILL START BY GIVING US THE SECRETS OF YOUR SPACESHIP. AND THEN YOU'LL TELL US ABOUT EARTH... AT LENGTH!

I WON'T TELL YOU ANYTHING!

COME, NOW. THERE'S NO SENSE IN RESISTING. THIS MACHINE ISN'T A TORTURE DEVICE. IT JUST MAKES PEOPLE TALK... BEGIN!!

26A

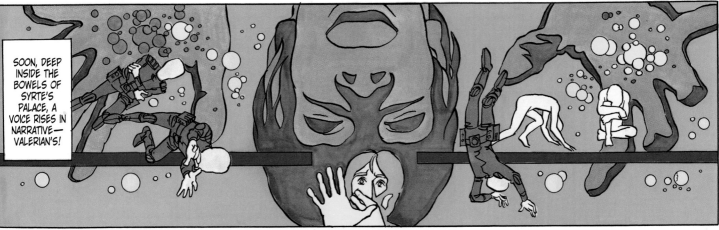

SOON, DEEP INSIDE THE BOWELS OF SYRTE'S PALACE, A VOICE RISES IN NARRATIVE— VALERIAN'S!

THE NEXT MORNING, IN THE NOW-EMPTY ROOM...

HOW HORRIBLE! I DON'T REMEMBER A THING. BUT I KNOW I TALKED... AND WHAT'S BECOME OF LAURELINE?

SUDDENLY, IN THE CORRIDOR...

26B

THIS IS THE PRISONER I TOLD YOU ABOUT, MY PRINCE. REMEMBER HOW YOU PROMISED ME YOU'D SET HIM FREE AND GRANT HIM YOUR PARDON...

AHEM, YES, OF COURSE... ER... GUARDS! FREE THIS PRISONER...

HIGHNESS! YOU CANNOT DO THIS. THIS BEING IS DANGEROUS. HE IS A THREAT TO YOUR EMPIRE...

REALLY? ER... IN THAT CASE, PERHAPS WE SHOULD WAIT TO...

27A

PRINCE! ARE YOU NO LONGER THE EMPEROR OF A THOUSAND PLANETS? ARE YOU GOING TO YIELD TO YOUR ADVISORS?!!

ER... NO, NO... OH, THIS MUST END! ALL THIS SHOUTING IS SO TIRESOME. LET THE PRISONER LEAVE WITH THIS GIRL, UNIMPEDED; I PROMISED... GUARDS! ESCORT THEM OUT! AND DO NOT BOTHER ME WITH THIS ANYMORE! I HAVE THE GREAT FESTIVAL OF STELLAR FLOWERS TO ORGANISE FOR TONIGHT, AFTER ALL...

AND WHILE THE PRINCE RETIRES...

VALERIAN IS SET FREE...

UNDER CLOSE WATCH, MARCHING BEFORE THE FROZEN ENLIGHTENEDS...

... THE TWO TERRANS ARE SOON BACK OUTSIDE THE PALACE DOORS...

LET'S PUT SOME DISTANCE BETWEEN THE ENLIGHTENEDS AND US QUICKLY. THEY SEEM PARALYSED FOR THE MOMENT, BUT IT WON'T LAST... AND TELL ME WHAT HAPPENED TO YOU...

CRAZY STORY! IT WAS THAT BLASTED SCHAMIR THAT MADE ME LOSE IT. I WAS STUCK AT THE BOTTOM OF THE HEAP AND COULDN'T BREATHE. IN THE END, I HAD TO BREAK IT TO GET OUT. AFTER THAT, I DON'T REALLY REMEMBER... EXCEPT THAT I ENDED UP INSIDE THE PRINCE'S LODGE. IN THE MORNING, A CALL FROM THE ENLIGHTENEDS INFORMED HIM THAT THEY'D CAPTURED AN IMPORTANT PRISONER...

IT DIDN'T TAKE ME LONG TO FIGURE OUT THAT IT WAS YOU. CONVINCING THE PRINCE WAS CHILD'S PLAY—HE'S A PUSHOVER... BUT HIS ORDERS ARE STILL SACRED. AT LEAST IN PRINCIPLE... THAT'S IT!

PIECE OF CAKE, INDEED! UNFORTUNATELY, I DON'T KNOW WHAT I MIGHT HAVE TOLD THE ENLIGHTENEDS LAST NIGHT. THE ONLY THING THAT'S CERTAIN IS THAT THEY CAN'T HAVE GOT INSIDE THE SHIP YET, SINCE THE LOCK IS SECURED BY A RETINAL SCAN...

ONLY ONE THING TO DO NOW. GET BACK TO ELMIR THE MERCHANT—OUR ONLY ALLY HERE... HEY, KID!! DO YOU KNOW BLACK STREET?

THAT WAY... YOU'VE GOT TO GO DOWN SOME MORE...

SOON, VALERIAN AND LAURELINE ARE WALKING THROUGH A VERITABLE CESSPOOL. LEANING AGAINST WALLS ROTTEN BY THE DAMP, LYING ON THE SLIMY GROUND, THE MISERABLE DREGS OF THE EMPIRE OF A THOUSAND PLANETS SEEM TO WAIT FOR WHO KNOWS WHAT, THEIR EYES EMPTY, UNRESPONSIVE...

SO THIS IS BLACK STREET!!!

YES... JUST LIKE ALL CAPITAL CITIES, SYRTE HAS ITS OWN SEEDY PARTS. LOOK! MANY OF THESE BEINGS HAVE BEEN IRRADIATED; OTHERS HAVE BEEN STRUCK WITH SPACE MADNESS... PERHAPS ONE OF THE POOR DEVILS WILL BE ABLE TO TAKE US TO ELMIR, ANYWAY...

SOME TIME LATER, AFTER A LONG WALK THROUGH DARK, LABYRINTHINE STREETS...

143

IT'S HERE, LORDS.

THANK YOU. HERE, TAKE THIS.

BAM BAM

WE'RE HERE TO SEE ELMIR THE MERCHANT. TELL HIM WE COME FROM THE PALACE, HE'LL UNDERSTAND.

AFTER A FEW MINUTES...

THIS IS THE GRANDMASTER OF THE MERCHANT GUILD.

?

YES, I DIDN'T TELL YOU THE WHOLE STORY...

... I MUST ALSO CONFESS THAT I'M SORRY TO RECEIVE YOU IN SUCH SQUALOR. BUT THIS IS THE ONLY DISTRICT WHERE THE ENLIGHTENEDS AND THEIR GOONS DON'T DARE GO... YOU'RE SAFE HERE...

BUT DO TELL ME HOW YOU GOT OUT OF THE PALACE WHILE I SHOW YOU TO OUR SECRET MEETING ROOM...

AT THE END OF A MAZE OF STAIRS AND CORRIDORS...

FRIENDS AND COLLEAGUES OF THE GUILD, HERE ARE THE TWO STRANGERS I TOLD YOU ABOUT...

... WE CAN TRUST THEM FOR THE MOMENT. AFTER ALL, THEY HAVE INCURRED THE ENLIGHTENEDS' HATRED, AND THAT'S SUFFICIENT GUARANTEE FOR ME. THEY'LL EXPLAIN WHAT THEY HAVE DISCOVERED. AFTER THAT... WELL, WE'LL SEE IF WE CAN WORK TOGETHER...

ALL RIGHT, LET ME BEGIN...

LATER, AFTER VALERIAN AND LAURELINE HAVE RECOUNTED THEIR ADVENTURES AND ANSWERED MANY QUESTIONS ON THE ENLIGHTENEDS' ACTIVITIES...

HMM... VERY INTERESTING. IT DIDN'T TAKE YOU LONG TO LEARN ALL OF THIS! YOUR INFORMATION CONFIRMS WHAT WE ALREADY SUSPECTED. BUT THERE ARE OTHER THINGS YOU MAY NOT BE AWARE OF...

THOSE ABANDONED LABORATORIES YOU SAW, THE OFF-LIMITS FACTORIES, THE CLOSED UNIVERSITIES... IT'S ALL THE WORK OF THE ENLIGHTENEDS. THEY APPEARED LESS THAN 100 YEARS AGO, AND SYRTE IS ALREADY GOING TO RUIN. KNOWLEDGE IS HUNTED DOWN. RELIGION REPLACES SCIENCE...

OUR SPACESHIPS ARE FALLING TO PIECES. THERE'S NO ONE LEFT TO REPAIR THEM...

AND THE SPACE ROUTES ARE SLOWLY FORGOTTEN BY BADLY TRAINED PILOTS.

144

BUT THE ENLIGHTENEDS DID MAKE A CONTRIBUTION, DIDN'T THEY?! THEIR POWERS ARE REAL—I'VE SEEN THEM AT WORK...

IT'S TRUE... THEIR MEDICAL AND PSYCHO-LOGICAL KNOWLEDGE IS MUCH MORE ADVANCED THAN SYRTE'S, WHERE THIS TYPE OF SCIENCE WAS NEVER OF MUCH INTEREST. IT IS THANKS TO THAT KNOWLEDGE THAT THEY GAINED THEIR HOLD ON THE PEOPLE AND THE NOBILITY...

BUT THEY'VE GAINED THEIR ASCENDAN-CY PRIMARILY BY RUTHLESSLY ELIMI-NATING ALL WHO OPPOSE THEM. WITH THE EMPEROR'S UNSPOKEN AGREEMENT, THEY KILL AND KIDNAP WITHOUT MERCY TO TAKE OVER ALL KEY POSITIONS.

THEY'VE EVEN STARTED GOING AFTER OUR SHIPS IN SPACE. MANY PLANETS HAVE STOPPED THEIR COMMERCIAL RELATIONS WITH US BECAUSE OF THEM. IT'S A DISASTER FOR THE GUILD!

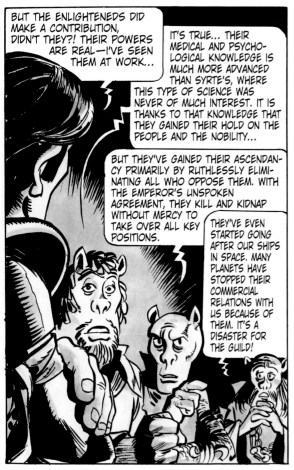

NOW YOU KNOW THE ESSENTIALS, AND WE HAVE A PROPOSITION FOR YOU. BUT I MUST FIRST WARN YOU THAT IF YOU BETRAY US, YOU'LL NEVER LEAVE SYRTE ALIVE! SO...

SO IT'S NOT LIKE WE HAVE MUCH CHOICE. ALONE, WE'LL NEVER MANAGE TO EVADE THE ENLIGHTENEDS. THEY MUST BE ON HIGH ALERT...

WHAT'S YOUR OFFER?

HERE'S HOW IT IS... WE'RE PREPARING AN EXPEDITION TO PUSH THE ENLIGHTENEDS OUT OF THEIR BASE. WE RECENTLY RECEIVED SOME INFORMATION, AND WE THINK WE KNOW MORE OR LESS WHERE THEIR LAIR IS. BUT WE LACK WEAPONS AND EXPERIENCE. I'VE SEEN YOUR SHIP... QUITE A MACHINE, NO DOUBT MORE IMPRESSIVE THAN OUR RICKETY OLD TRANSPORTS. WILL YOU TAKE COMMAND OF THE CONVOY WITH ME? SEVERAL PLANETS FEAR SEEING SYRTE REVERT BACK TO THE DARK AGES AND ARE READY TO FOLLOW US. THEY ONLY WAIT FOR OUR SIGNAL TO SEND US THEIR BEST SHIPS. IN EXCHANGE FOR YOUR HELP, WE OFFER YOU PROTECTION AGAINST THE ENLIGHTENEDS AND A WAY TO RETAKE YOUR OWN SHIP. NOT TO MENTION OUR PROMISE THAT YOU CAN LEAVE FREELY ONCE YOUR MISSION IS COMPLETE.

ALL RIGHT, I ACCEPT! WHEN ARE YOU PLANNING TO LEAVE SYRTE?

30.A

IN A FEW DAYS. WE JUST NEED TO COMPLETE OUR PREPARATIONS. I'LL GIVE YOU THE DETAILS OF THE PLAN ONCE WE'RE UNDERWAY. IN THE MEANTIME, YOU'D PROBABLY LIKE TO GET SOME REST?

NOT LIKE IT'D BE WISE TO GO OUT FOR A WALK INSTEAD.

AND...

YOUR CHAMBERS! CONSIDER YOURSELF AT HOME... WELL... SO TO SPEAK... BECAUSE... ERM... ACTUALLY, WHERE EXACTLY IS HOME?

TSK, TSK... DON'T BE TOO CURIOUS, ELMIR!

DON'T WORRY, LAURELINE. I'M SURE THE GUILD UNDERSTANDS THE NEED FOR SECRECY IN BUSINESS MATTERS...

THREE DAYS LATER...

OH, OH! THE PEACEFUL MER-CHANTS OF THE GUILD, NOW TURNED MIGHTY WARRIORS!

WHAT CAN I SAY? I'D MUCH RATHER BE RUNNING MY BUSINESS IN PEACE. BUT I DON'T EVEN GO OUT WITHOUT BODYGUARDS ANYMORE. THE ENLIGH-TENEDS HAVE SCOURED THE ENTIRE CITY TO FIND YOU, AND THE SPACEPORT IS FULL OF SPIES.

ANYWAY... WE'RE READY! THE TOUGHEST PART COMES NOW...

WITH THE SIMPLEST PLAN OF ALL: OPENLY AND IN BROAD DAYLIGHT, AS YOU'LL SEE! HA! HA! LET'S GO— THEY'RE WAITING FOR US.

HOW ARE YOU GOING TO PROCEED?

30.B

SOON, DOWN IN THE SLUMS OF SYRTE, A MARCH BEGINS. AT EACH CROSSROAD, A NEW CONTINGENT OF GUILD MEMBERS JOINS THE PROCESSION...

ON THE DOCKS, THE CROWD IS EVEN THICKER...

WELL DONE, ELMIR!

NOT BAD, IT'S TRUE... BUT MAKE NO MISTAKE: FLUNKIES OF THE ENLIGHTENEDS ARE LYING IN WAIT EVERYWHERE. KEEP YOUR HEADS DOWN FOR THE CROSSING...

WHEN THEY ARRIVE AT THE SPACEPORT, IT IS AN ENORMOUS CROWD THAT ESCORTS VALERIAN AND LAURELINE TO THEIR SHIP. UNABLE TO DO A THING, THE GUARDS WATCH FROM THE SIDELINES...

THAT'S IT! WE'RE THROUGH!

YES. AND THE THREE SHIPS IMMEDIATELY AROUND YOURS WILL COME WITH US. THEY BELONG TO THE GUILD. OTHERS WILL JOIN US ALONG THE WAY.

EVERYTHING LOOKS INTACT; THEY COULDN'T GET PAST THE LOCK. GET IN, QUICK!

I HAVE AN OLD MAP OF THE SYRTIAN SYSTEM WITH ME. ONE OF THE FEW COMPLETE ONES...

AND SOON, IN SYRTE'S SERENE SKY...

... MOST OF THE EMPIRE'S ARCHIVES HAVE VANISHED IN THE PAST FEW YEARS—WHAT A COINCIDENCE—TO THE POINT THAT THERE ARE MANY PLANETS NOW FORGOTTEN ALTOGETHER... FOR THE MOMENT, HEAD TOWARDS THE CONSTELLATION OF THE EAGLE. I'LL GIVE YOU THE COURSE CORRECTIONS LATER, ONCE OUR CONVOY IS ASSEMBLED.

UNDERSTOOD. LET'S GO... LAURELINE, CALL THE OTHERS AND GIVE THEM THE FOLLOWING VECTORS...

146

EVERYWHERE WITHIN THE EMPIRE OF A THOUSAND PLANETS, NEWS OF THE EXPEDITION'S DEPARTURE REACHES THOSE WHO HAVE BEEN WAITING FOR THAT MOMENT, SOMETIMES FOR YEARS. IN THE SECRET CODE OF THE MERCHANT GUILD, RENDEZVOUS POINTS IN SPACE ARE SET...

FROM MURMYL, HOME OF THE SYSTEM'S GREATEST ARCHITECTS...

FROM THE FOREST PLANET GLAM, WITH ITS FREEDOM-LOVING POPU-LATION...

FROM THE POWERFUL INDUS-TRIAL CENTRE OF MINTEL...

COME IN... THE GUILD IS CALLING ITS REPRESENTATIVE ON SIMIUS... JOIN US AT THE AGREED-UPON COORDINATES...

FROM EVERY WORLD WHERE THE YOKE OF THE ENLIGHTENEDS HAS BROUGHT ITS LOT OF VICTIMS, BROKEN A CULTURE OR SMOTHERED A TRADE, PEOPLE TAKE OFF TO JOIN THE CRUSADE...

32

A POWERFUL CONVOY IS SLOWLY PUT TOGETHER. ALMOST IMPERCEPTIBLY, IT STRAYS OFF THE TRADE ROUTES AND PLUNGES INTO DEEP SPACE. HOURS PASS BY SLOWLY...

IN VALERIAN'S SHIP, WHERE—AT ELMIR'S REQUEST—EVERYTHING IS READY TO FACE POSSIBLE COMBAT...

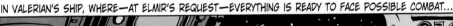

MY FRIENDS, WE'RE NEARING OUR OBJECTIVE. THE TIME HAS COME TO EXPLAIN OUR PLAN TO YOU. LOOK AT THE MAP: THIS IS SLOHM, A DUSTBALL ASTEROID CHARTED BY OUR SCOUTS MANY MILLENNIA AGO, AND COMPLETELY ABANDONED SINCE...

A POOR WRETCH WHO WAS BEING KEPT PRISONER THERE BY THE ENLIGHTENEDS MANAGED TO ESCAPE BY HIDING ABOARD ONE OF THEIR CRAFT... BEFORE HE DIED, SHORTLY AFTER REACHING SYRTE, HE REVEALED THAT A GIGANTIC SHIPWRECK ON THE SURFACE SERVED AS THE ENLIGHTENEDS' BASE. FROM THERE, THEY CONTROL ALL THEIR EMISSARIES ON OTHER PLANETS.

THEY ALSO ESTABLISHED SOME SORT OF LABOUR CAMP. THE PRISONERS, WATCHED BY ARMED GUARDS, SEEM TO BE WORKING TO SUSTAIN THEIR MASTERS...

AND YOU WANT TO STRIKE AT THE HEAD, TO DEPRIVE THE ENLIGHTENEDS SCATTERED AROUND THE SYSTEM OF A RALLYING POINT! RISKY, BUT IF IT WORKS...

SO, IN OTHER WORDS, WE'RE FLYING STRAIGHT INTO THE LION'S DEN!! BUT, SURELY SLOHM IS WELL DEFENDED?

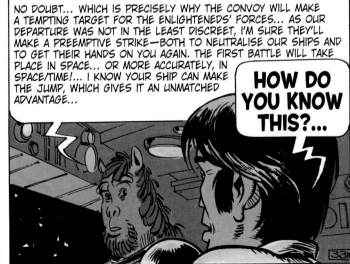

NO DOUBT... WHICH IS PRECISELY WHY THE CONVOY WILL MAKE A TEMPTING TARGET FOR THE ENLIGHTENEDS' FORCES... AS OUR DEPARTURE WAS NOT IN THE LEAST DISCREET, I'M SURE THEY'LL MAKE A PREEMPTIVE STRIKE—BOTH TO NEUTRALISE OUR SHIPS AND TO GET THEIR HANDS ON YOU AGAIN. THE FIRST BATTLE WILL TAKE PLACE IN SPACE... OR MORE ACCURATELY, IN SPACE/TIME!... I KNOW YOUR SHIP CAN MAKE THE JUMP, WHICH GIVES IT AN UNMATCHED ADVANTAGE...

HOW DO YOU KNOW THIS?...

EASY TO FIGURE OUT. TO START WITH, YOU'RE THE FIRST STRANGERS TO VISIT THE SYRTIAN SYSTEM— AS YOUR DISASTROUS IGNORANCE OF OUR CUSTOMS PROVES. BESIDES, WHAT ELSE WOULD ALL THESE EXTRA INSTRUMENTS ON YOUR BRIDGE BE FOR?

NO NEED! BACK WHEN THERE WAS STILL SCIENTIFIC RESEARCH DONE ON SYRTE, OUR ASTRONOMERS HAD QUITE THE REPUTATION... I DABBLED IN SUCH THINGS MYSELF IN MY YOUTH. YOU COME FROM THE SOL SYSTEM! JUDGING BY YOUR PHYSICAL CONFIGURATION, I'D EVEN SAY THE THIRD PLANET...

TOUCHÉ... I WAS ABOUT TO TELL YOU, ANYWAY... I THINK IT'S ALSO TIME FOR US TO TELL YOU WHERE WE COME FROM...

TOUCHÉ AGAIN! BUT HOW DID YOU...

THE TIMEPIECE, OF COURSE! I WAS IN THE CROWD WHEN YOU FIRST ENCOUNTERED AN ENLIGHTENED. I ASKED A FEW QUESTIONS OF THE COLLEAGUE WHO SOLD YOU THE ITEM IN QUESTION. I LEARNED A LOT ABOUT ITS ORIGIN...

AND IT'S THE STRANGEST THING: THAT WATCH, AS YOU CALL IT, WAS EXCHANGED FOR SOME JEWELLERY BY AN ENLIGHTENED... WHICH WOULD TEND TO MEAN THAT...

VALERIAN! DISTRESS CALL FROM THE GLAM SHIP! THEY'RE UNDER ATTACK!!!

HERE WE GO... THE TRAP IS SPRUNG—EVEN EARLIER THAN WE THOUGHT...

YES... THE QUESTION NOW IS: WHO'S CAUGHT IN IT?

34A

IN AN INSTANT, THE ENLIGHTENEDS' SHIPS APPEAR OUT OF NOWHERE AND OPEN FIRE ON THE CONVOY WITH DEADLY ACCURACY. BUT THEIR TARGETS, ON ALERT, RETURN FIRE WITH EQUAL RUTHLESS- NESS. IN THE BLAZE OF THERMAL SHIELDS, IN THE CHAOS OF CRISSCROSSING VIDEO CALLS...

... VALERIAN, WHO HAS TAKEN THE HELM OF HIS SHIP, IS ABOUT TO JOIN THE FIGHT...

I MUST WARN YOU, ELMIR! THE FIRST JUMP IS ALWAYS A SERIOUS SHOCK—AND WE'RE ABOUT TO CHAIN SEVERAL HERE. EVEN LAURELINE AND I CAN'T BE CERTAIN OF SURVIVING IT...

I HAVE FAITH! THE FUTURE OF SYRTE IS AT STAKE!

THEN, DIVING INTO SPACE/TIME...

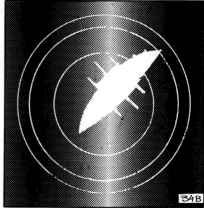

34B

149

... THE TERRAN SHIP MATERIALISES IN QUICK SUCCESSION AT KEY POINTS OF THE BATTLE. IN A FEW MILLIONTHS OF A SECOND, IT CONDUCTS A SERIES OF SPACE/TIME JUMPS WITH PERFECT PRECISION...

IN THE SILENCE OF SPACE, THE INESCAPABLE SALVOES OF ITS MOLECULAR CANNONS CREATE A SINGLE, BLINDING FLASH OF LIGHT... INSTANTLY TURNING THE TIDE OF THE BATTLE IN FAVOUR OF THE GUILD.

35

FLOATING ADRIFT AMONG THE CHARRED REMNANTS OF THE ENLIGHTENEDS' VESSELS, VALERIAN'S SHIP IS BROUGHT TO A STOP BY HIS EXHAUSTED PILOT. AS SUDDENLY AS IT HAD BEGUN, THE BATTLE IS OVER. AND WHILE, IN THE DISTANCE, THE PARTLY-DECIMATED CONVOY CONTINUES ON ITS WAY...

... I'M SO DEADLY TIRED... FEEL LIKE I'VE JUST AGED A CENTURY... WHAT ABOUT LAURELINE?... ELMIR?...

PHEWWW... YOU TOOK SOME INSANE RISKS... HOW'S ELMIR?...

HE'S STARTING TO COME TO. CALL THE OTHER SHIPS AND TELL THEM TO HEAD STRAIGHT FOR SLOHM. WE HAVE TO MAINTAIN THE ELEMENT OF SURPRISE...

ABOVE SLOHM, A GHOST CONVOY PREPARES TO LAND...

SOON...

WE'RE NEARING SLOHM... I LOCATED THE LABOUR CAMP AND THE ENLIGHTENEDS' VESSEL. NO SIGN OF ANY REACTION YET... THAT'S WEIRD...

HMM... WE'LL LAND SOME DISTANCE FROM THE CAMP. ASK THE CONVOY TO FLY IN CLOSE FORMATION AROUND US, AND SWITCH ON THE CLOAKING FIELD. WE'LL BE PROTECTED FROM SIGHT AND RADAR FOR THE LANDING...

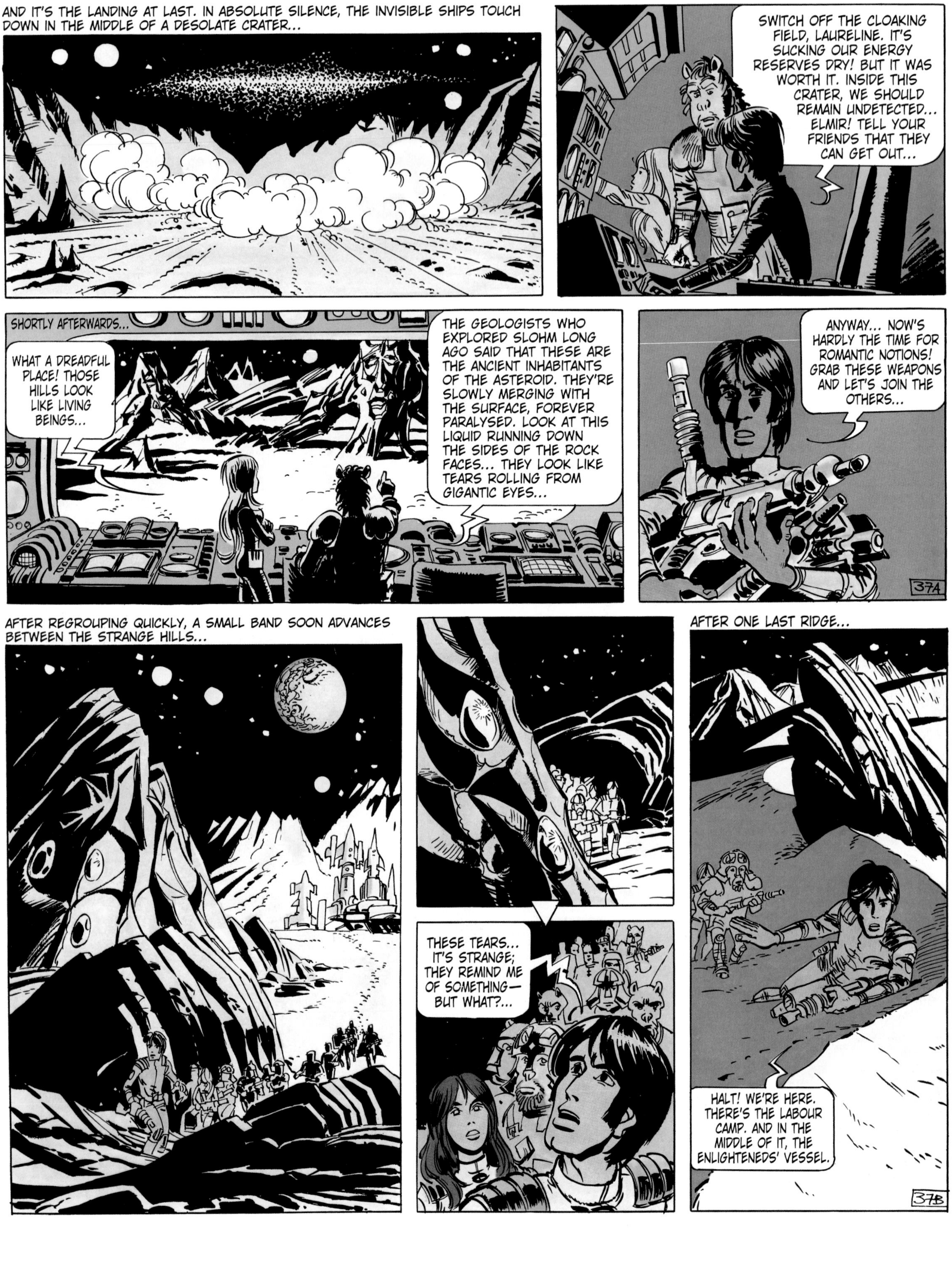
AND IT'S THE LANDING AT LAST. IN ABSOLUTE SILENCE, THE INVISIBLE SHIPS TOUCH DOWN IN THE MIDDLE OF A DESOLATE CRATER...
SWITCH OFF THE CLOAKING FIELD, LAURELINE. IT'S SUCKING OUR ENERGY RESERVES DRY! BUT IT WAS WORTH IT. INSIDE THIS CRATER, WE SHOULD REMAIN UNDETECTED... ELMIR! TELL YOUR FRIENDS THAT THEY CAN GET OUT...
SHORTLY AFTERWARDS...
WHAT A DREADFUL PLACE! THOSE HILLS LOOK LIKE LIVING BEINGS...
THE GEOLOGISTS WHO EXPLORED SLOHM LONG AGO SAID THAT THESE ARE THE ANCIENT INHABITANTS OF THE ASTEROID. THEY'RE SLOWLY MERGING WITH THE SURFACE, FOREVER PARALYSED. LOOK AT THIS LIQUID RUNNING DOWN THE SIDES OF THE ROCK FACES... THEY LOOK LIKE TEARS ROLLING FROM GIGANTIC EYES...
ANYWAY... NOW'S HARDLY THE TIME FOR ROMANTIC NOTIONS! GRAB THESE WEAPONS AND LET'S JOIN THE OTHERS...
37A
AFTER REGROUPING QUICKLY, A SMALL BAND SOON ADVANCES BETWEEN THE STRANGE HILLS...
THESE TEARS... IT'S STRANGE; THEY REMIND ME OF SOMETHING— BUT WHAT?...
AFTER ONE LAST RIDGE...
HALT! WE'RE HERE. THERE'S THE LABOUR CAMP. AND IN THE MIDDLE OF IT, THE ENLIGHTENEDS' VESSEL.
37B

LET'S SPLIT UP. WE'RE GOING TO HAVE TO TAKE THE GUARDS BY SURPRISE IF WE WANT TO AVOID CAUSING A MASSACRE OF THE PRISONERS.

VERY WELL. I'LL SPLIT US INTO FOUR GROUPS AND GET THEM INTO POSITION AROUND THE CRATER... YOU'LL GIVE THE SIGNAL TO ATTACK BY FIRING THE FIRST SHOT.

ALL RIGHT. MAKE SURE YOU DON'T GIVE THEM TIME TO FIRE BACK...

IN SMALL GROUPS, THE GUILD'S TROOPS SCATTER THROUGH THE SHADOWS. SILENCE STILL REIGNS OVER THE CAMP, ONLY BROKEN BY THE OCCASIONAL CRACK OF A WHIP OR HOARSE SCREAM WHEN A PRISONER IS TARGETED BY A GUARD. THE POOR WRETCHES CLIMB ONTO RICKETY PLATFORMS TO GATHER THE PHOSPHORESCENT LIQUID THAT FLOWS SPARINGLY DOWN THE ROCK. BUCKETS PASS FROM HAND TO HAND. NOT A WORD IS EXCHANGED, NOT A LAMENT IS HEARD... AN OPPRESSIVE, HOPE-CRUSHING ROUTINE SEEMS TO PERMEATE EVERY GESTURE...

SUDDENLY...

153

COMPLETE CHAOS SOON OVERTAKES THE ENTIRE CAMP. LEAVING THEIR POSTS NEAR THE ENLIGHTENEDS' VESSEL, MORE GUARDS JUMP INTO THE FRAY— BUT IN VAIN.

HELPED BY THE PRISONERS, WHO HAVE QUICKLY SEIZED ON THE EXTRAORDINARY CHANCE GIVEN TO THEM...

... LED BY VALERIAN AND LAURELINE...

... THE GUILD'S FIGHTERS STORM THE CAMP AND TAKE IT.

SOON AFTER, MORNING COMES TO THE ASTEROID. THE FORMER PRISONERS AND THEIR LIBERATORS STAND BEFORE THE MASSIVE SHIPWRECK ON SLOHM'S SURFACE...

NO REACTION FROM THE ENLIGHTENEDS... THIS IS STRANGE...

FACING THE ENORMOUS, STILL STRUCTURE, THE BESIEGERS ARE GRIPPED BY INDECISION.

WHAT DO WE DO NOW?

HMM... I WONDER WHAT THIS SILENCE CAN MEAN. WE SHOULD GO IN AND SEE...

DON'T GO INSIDE THIS SHIP. EVEN THE GUARDS NEVER DID. THEY SAY IT'S CERTAIN DEATH FOR ANY WHO VENTURE INSIDE...

EARTHLING! WE'RE WAITING FOR YOU ABOARD. YOU ALONE! YOU WILL BE SAFE.

I'M COMING!

WHEN VALERIAN ENTERS THE SPACESHIP, HE IS GREETED BY SCENES OF DESOLATION. ABANDONED HYDROPONICS PLANTATIONS GROWN OUT OF CONTROL...

... HUMAN AND ANIMAL SKELETONS...

... RUINED ENGINES AND GUTTED WALLS...

WHEN HE FINALLY REACHES THE COCKPIT...

HERE I AM... I'M VALERIAN. AND YOU, WHO ARE YOU?

HUMANS, LIKE YOU!... OR, MORE ACCURATELY, WHAT'S LEFT OF THEM!...

GAZE UPON US, SINCE YOU WANT TO KNOW WHAT WE LOOK LIKE!

I... I DON'T UNDERSTAND...

WHEN YOU GET BACK TO EARTH, YOU CAN CONSULT THE ARCHIVES OF THAT NEW CAPITAL YOU SPOKE OF TO OUR BROTHERS AT THE IMPERIAL PALACE... THE GALAXITY THAT SENT YOU... YOU WILL DISCOVER THAT A GIANT SHIP, CARRYING ALL THE HOPES OF THE HUMAN RACE, LEFT THE MOTHER PLANET CENTURIES AGO.

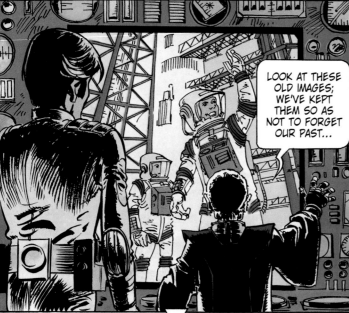

LOOK AT THESE OLD IMAGES; WE'VE KEPT THEM SO AS NOT TO FORGET OUR PAST...

BUT... SEVERAL MISSIONS WERE SENT TO FIND THIS SHIP SINCE THE ADVENT OF THE SPACE/TIME JUMP! IT WAS BELIEVED THAT IT HAD DISAPPEARED WITH ALL HANDS IN SOME SORT OF COSMIC DISASTER...

IT WASN'T COMPLETELY DESTROYED. BUT WE WERE BLOWN OFF COURSE BY STELLAR WINDS AND DRIFTED TOWARDS THE SYRTIAN SYSTEM. THE HULL WAS BREACHED IN SEVERAL PLACES, AND MOST OF US DIED FROM RADIA-TION. THE OTHERS HAD BARELY ENOUGH STRENGTH LEFT TO GUIDE THE STRICKEN SHIP TO THIS GODFORSAKEN ASTEROID, WHERE IT FINALLY CRASHED FOR GOOD...

OUR VESSEL WAS CREWED BY THE BEST SCIENTISTS AT THE TIME. IT WAS SUPPOSED TO SEEK NEW WORLDS TO REPLACE EARTH, WHICH WAS DYING, ITS SURFACE DEVASTATED BY NUCLEAR EXPLOSIONS... I WAS ITS CAPTAIN...

THOSE WHO WERE LEFT OWED THEIR SURVIVAL TO THE PHOSPHORESCENT TEARS WE COLLECTED FROM SLOHM... OUR EQUIPMENT HAD DETECTED THE PRESENCE OF THIS POWERFUL ANTIDOTE TO THE AILMENTS OF SPACE... OUR DOCTORS TURNED IT INTO A TRUE ELIXIR OF IMMORTALITY.

THAT BREW I SAW THEM DRINK ON SYRTE! SO THIS IS HOW THESE POOR WRETCHES SURVIVED ALL THIS TIME.

THREE CENTURIES PASSED BEFORE WE COULD CAPTURE A SYRTIAN SPACESHIP THAT HAD LANDED ON SLOHM AFTER AN EMERGENCY. THEN, SOME OF US LEFT THIS ACCURSED ROCK TO COLONISE SYRTE. NOW KNOWN AS THE ENLIGHTENEDS, WE FOUNDED A RELIGION AND INFILTRATED THE SYSTEM'S POWER STRUCTURE. ONCE IT WAS COMPLETELY UNDER OUR CONTROL, WE WERE TO USE THE RICHES OF THE EMPIRE TO RETURN TO EARTH IN A POSITION OF STRENGTH.

WHY MOUNT SUCH AN EXPEDITION?

DON'T YOU UNDERSTAND? THE EARTH TURNED US INTO COSMIC MONSTROSITIES!

BEINGS SUSTAINED ONLY BY THE THOUGHT OF TAKING REVENGE AGAINST THEIR MOTHER PLANET!

... IMMORTALS WITHOUT A REASON TO LIVE!

COME BACK TO EARTH! YOU'LL BE TREATED AS HEROES!

IMPOSSIBLE! WE'RE JUST HOMELESS TRASH NOW. AND YET, YOUR ARRIVAL HAD GIVEN RISE TO SUCH HIGH HOPES IN US. WE THOUGHT WE WOULD EXTRACT THE SECRET OF SPACE/TIME TRAVEL FROM YOU. BUT YOU KEPT EVADING US. IN THE END, WE ONLY SUCCEEDED IN LOSING EVERY LAST ONE OF OUR SHIPS IN YESTERDAY'S BATTLE— WE THREW EVERYTHING WE HAD AT YOU...

WE CANNOT COMPETE WITH THE TERRIFYING WEAPONS OF TODAY'S EARTH. AND WE BELONG NEITHER ON OUR WORLD, WHERE WE ARE FORGOTTEN, NOR ON SYRTE, WHERE WE'RE HATED. SO WE'VE MADE OUR DECISION...

WHAT DO YOU MEAN?

IN EXACTLY FIVE MINUTES, THIS WRECK WILL BLOW UP—AND US WITH IT!

TAKE THIS. YOU CAN USE IT AS PROOF OF OUR EXISTENCE WHEN YOU TELL OUR PATHETIC TALE...

THE WATCH WE FOUND IN SYRTE'S MARKET!

42-A

INDEED... IT BELONGED TO ONE OF US... TIME, ALWAYS THE OBSESSION OF MEN... GOODBYE NOW, EARTHLING. WE HAVE NOTHING LEFT TO SAY, AND THE SHIP WILL EXPLODE VERY SOON...

AND...

TAKE COVER! IT'S GONNA BLOW!!!

42-B

A FEW DAYS LATER, AS THE GUILD'S CONVOY IS HEADING BACK TO SYRTE, CARRYING SLOHM'S FORMER PRISONERS...

IT'S ALL OVER, VALERIAN. I CALLED THE REPRESENTATIVES OF THE GUILD THROUGHOUT THE EMPIRE. EVERYWHERE, WHEN THEY HEARD THAT SLOHM HAD FALLEN, THE LAST ENLIGHTENEDS BLEW THEMSELVES UP WITH THEIR TEMPLES. A TERRIBLE END, BUT MAYBE IT HAD TO BE THIS WAY...

NOW THAT THE DANGER IS GONE, EVERYTHING WILL GO BACK TO THE WAY IT WAS... AH! THE MERCHANT GUILD WILL ONCE AGAIN DO GREAT THINGS! THINGS HAPPENED SO FAST, THANKS TO YOUR HELP, VALERIAN... IT'S HARD TO BELIEVE...

YOU'RE RIGHT NOT TO BELIEVE IT TOO EASILY, ELMIR. DO YOU REALLY THINK THINGS WILL REVERT TO WHAT THEY WERE?

WHAT DO YOU MEAN?

I'VE RECEIVED SOME NEWS TOO. WHILE YOU WERE PLACING YOUR CALLS, LAURELINE MANAGED TO CONTACT THE CAPITAL...

THE REVOLUTION HAS BEGUN ON SYRTE!

THE FISHERMEN, THE FARMERS, THE CRAFTSMEN... THEY'RE STORMING THE PALACE... LONG-FORGOTTEN TEACHERS, EXILED SCIENTISTS HAVE COME OUT OF HIDING TO LEAD THE REVOLT... OTHER PLANETS ARE RISING UP TOO. EVERYWHERE, THE IMPERIAL ARISTOCRACY IS THREATENED...

SERIOUSLY, ELMIR... HOW DO YOU EXPLAIN THE EASE WITH WHICH THE ENLIGHTENEDS TOOK OVER THE EMPIRE? IT WAS BECAUSE IT WAS ALREADY SICK... TOO MANY PARTIES AND WEALTH ON ONE SIDE, TOO MUCH MISERY AND IGNORANCE ON THE OTHER...

THE MERCHANT GUILD THOUGHT IT WAS A VOICE OF REBELLION, BUT IT'S BEEN OVERTAKEN BY THE SUCCESS OF ITS OWN RAID. FEAR OF THE ENLIGHTENEDS WAS THE LOCK THAT KEPT THE IMPERIAL SYSTEM IN PLACE. WHEN YOU REMOVED IT, YOU RELEASED OTHER FORCES...

ERM... I DON'T REALLY MIND, TO BE HONEST. WHATEVER REGIME REPLACES OUR DYNASTY OF HALFWITS, THEY'LL HAVE NEED OF CLEVER PEOPLE... SAY... IF WE LEFT THAT CONVOY OF SLOWPOKES BEHIND AND JUMPED, WE COULD ARRIVE AT SYRTE IMMEDIATELY, COULDN'T WE?...

HA, HA... OF COURSE...

THEN, WHAT ARE WE WAITING FOR?...

AND, DIVING ONCE AGAIN INTO SPACE/TIME...

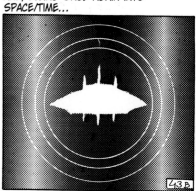

... THE TERRAN SHIP MATERIALISES ABOVE SYRTE'S SPACEPORT, WHERE THE BATTLE RAGES...

SOON...

THOSE HOTHEADS ARE AS BAD AS YOU WERE ABOUT GETTING INTO THE PALACE...

... A GOOD THING ELMIR HAS A FEW IDEAS ABOUT HOW TO DO SO DISCREETLY. YOU NEVER KNOW... IT MIGHT BE A GOOD THING TO BE AMONG THE FIRST INSIDE—IN CASE OF PROVISIONAL GOVERNMENTS, THAT SORT OF THING, YOU KNOW! GOODBYE, FRIENDS... AND DON'T FORGET: ONCE I'M IN POWER, I'LL BE COMPLETELY OPEN TO TRADE RELATIONS BETWEEN EARTH AND SYRTE!!

GOODBYE, ELMIR!

GOOD OLD, CYNICAL ELMIR! I LIKED HIM, THOUGH...

WE'LL SEE HIM AGAIN... NO DOUBT EARTH WILL SEND A LARGE-SCALE MISSION TO SYRTE ONCE WE TURN IN OUR REPORT. BUT, FOR THE MOMENT, THEY DON'T NEED US HERE ANYMORE. WE'RE GOING HOME.

STORY: P. CHRISTIN
DRAWING: J.C. MEZIERES
1970

THE END

159

VALERIAN

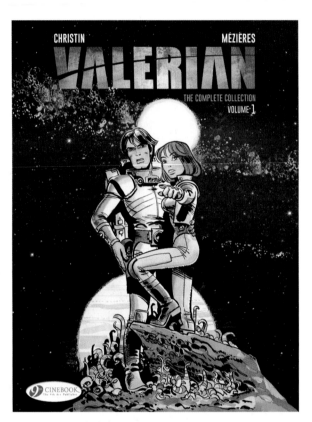

COMING SOON

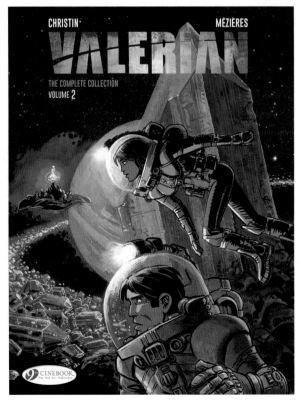

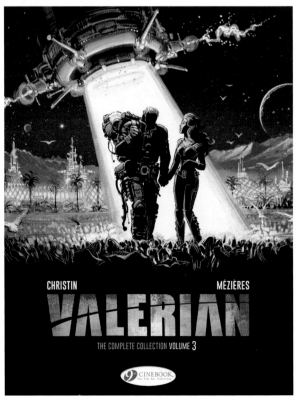

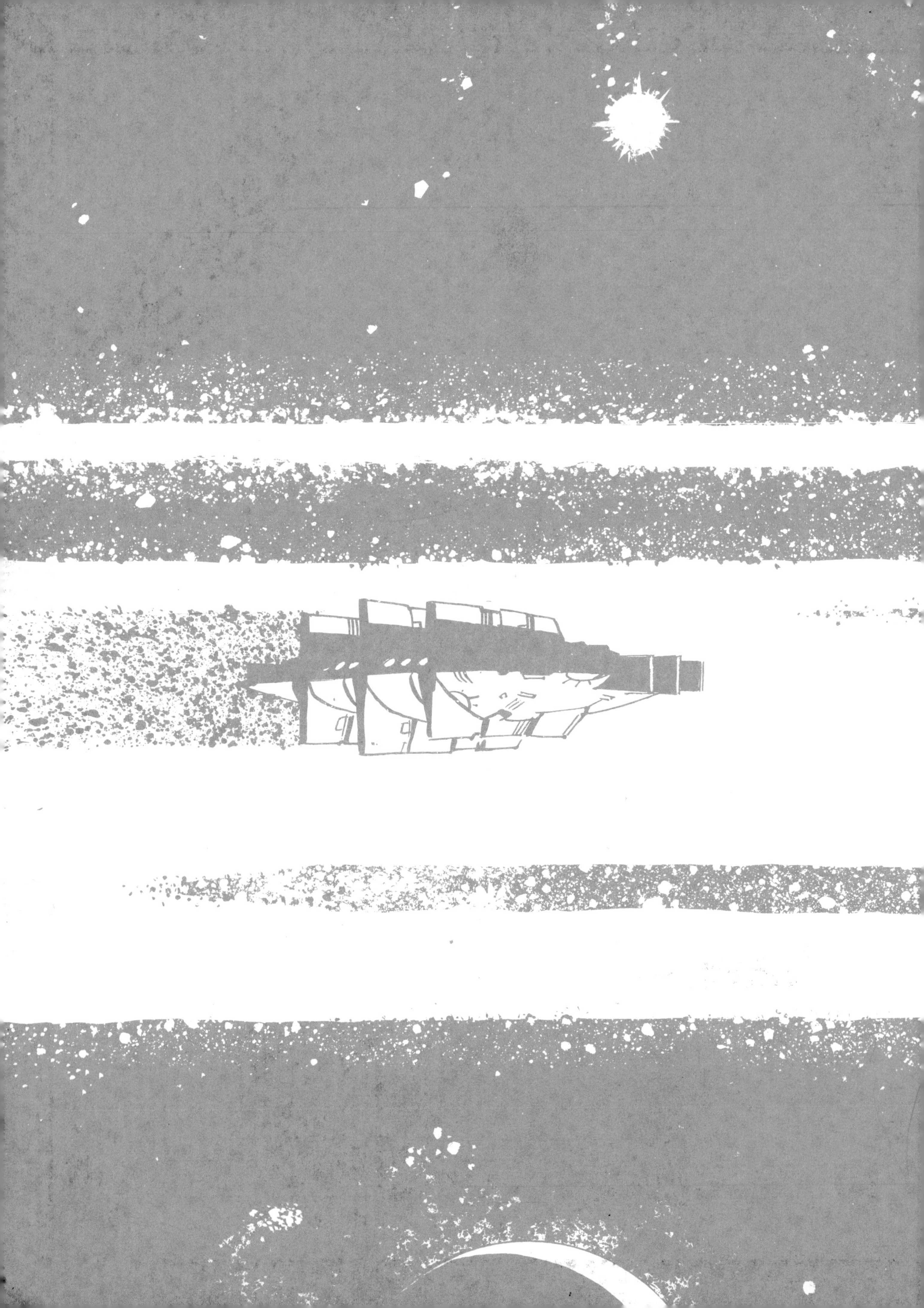